# A Diagram of God's Love

*Interior illustrations by John Collins*
*Floral motif on cover and throughout interior is taken from the design of one of the stained glass windows at Holy Trinity Brompton, where John was vicar from 1980 to 1985.*

Published by Alpha International
HTB Brompton Road
London SW7 1JA
Email: publications@alpha.org
Website: alpha.org

# A Diagram of God's Love

## *Experiencing His Infinite Love For Us*

### JOHN COLLINS

# Contents

# Introduction

If you suspect that there is more in the Christian faith than you have yet found out, I hope that you will read this book. The *Diagram* is an introduction to Christianity, a bird's-eye view of what it's all about and, perhaps to your surprise, what it's *not* all about.

I often think that Christianity is like King's College, Cambridge. From a distance, the chapel has a striking silhouette of ancient grey walls, of strange little towers and pinnacles, for all the world (as the Cambridgeshire farmers say) like a sow on its back. But then we enter, passing through the west door. And nothing has prepared us for the glory of the interior: the fan vault floating high above us, the sun shining through the great south windows – each one glowing with the deep blues, reds, greens and gold of seventeenth-century glass.

So it is with Christianity. There is *an outside*. We learn about outside-Christianity from countless sources: from history, art, or from doing an A-level in religious studies. There is also *an inside*. The *Diagram* is an attempt to introduce inside-Christianity – but still only an introduction.

Having said that, I hope that you will come to see that the five events traced out by the diagram are far, far more than an introduction. They underpin the greatest blessings and joys of the Christian life. We need, therefore, to discover them for ourselves, and then to hold strongly to them until our dying day. They will keep us safe in 'many a danger, toil, and snare',[1] and, they will uphold us through the sorrows and battles that no Christian can hope to escape.

In writing this book, I have often thought of another one, much thicker, that was recommended to me when I was a student. In the opening pages, there was a footnote. With a rather endearing arrogance the author wrote, 'At the first reading of my book ...' This was followed a few pages later by another footnote, 'At the second reading of my book ...' On this, I remember murmuring, 'You'll be lucky!'

Were I to follow that author's example, I might say, 'At the first reading of my book (if you enjoy it, as I hope you will), I would expect you to read quickly.' But, when you come to the last page, although I would never dream of recommending a second reading, I would certainly want you *to pause*. And not only to pause, but to look back at the five main chapters, and to ask yourself, 'Should I return to the "believing pages" and spend more time on them?'

So, what are these believing pages? In the middle of the eighteenth century, some Christians held 'Believing Meetings'. In these gatherings, they didn't teach. They didn't study. They didn't ask God for this and that. There wasn't even any singing until they were about to go home. Instead, they spent the time looking at some great promise of God, meditating upon it, and learning how to rest their faith on it. This was a brilliant idea. I have tried to revive this brainchild by placing a believing page at the end of each chapter. When you reach a believing page, please don't hurry on to the next chapter, or even peep at it. Stop! Think over the promise. Spend time with it. Ask yourself: 'Do I understand it?' If the answer is 'yes', pray the prayer(s). Then turn your prayers into praise: true praise is faith and love expressed.

One more thing that I hope you will keep in mind as you read. As you will see, I have attached a diagram to these wonderful themes. But, of course, there is no blessing in a diagram unless it clarifies Christ's stupendous achievements. So if the diagram of God's love helps *you*, and also lends wings to the task of sharing that love with a friend, use and study it prayerfully. If it doesn't, put a line through it, and write over it the single word: 'JESUS'. After all, the only purpose of this diagram is to encourage us to 'pass through' the printed page – even to pass through the promises of God – and to embrace our living Lord and Saviour, Jesus Christ, and to walk side by side with him forever.

As a would-be writer, I am haunted by the report of a Christian meeting that appeared in the columns of a provincial newspaper. The final sentence read, 'At the end of the evening, after the speaker had retired from the platform, a large crow was left in the town hall, singing the hymn "Abide with me".'[2]

I am, therefore, immensely grateful to Martin Peppiatt and to my brother-in-law, Andrew Kimpton. They have both spent countless hours reading my manuscript with kindly patience, eliminating sloppy writing, spotting 'monstrous crows' and making wise suggestions. Then, again, my profound gratitude to three other friends: Nicky Gumbel, who self-sacrificially included the manuscript in his *holiday* reading and sent me an email with his all-too-generous reaction, now appearing on the back cover; Nicky Lee, who read an early draft and greatly encouraged me, strengthening my feeble knees for the long journey to publication; Roger Wagner, who perused the final draft, his pencil, as ever, sensitively poised, and who made four valuable comments. Also it would be quite wrong for me not to mention those who, over the years, have cheered me on: David Smith, one-time colleague, who, to my great benefit, has often reminded me of the acronym of KISS.[3] Guy Gross, headmaster, who asked me to write some of this book fifty years ago and has regularly and patiently inquired about its progress – 'Collins, where is your prep? I am waiting for it.' I scarcely dare hand it in so late. And, more recently, my near neighbour, Joanne Williams, who read the early pages, lent me her great expertise, and, whenever we met, encouraged me to persist.

This brings me to my publishers. I was apprehensive about meeting my Editorial Manager, Miranda Lever, and the rest of the team, including Pete Bellenger and Katherine Blake. How wrong one can be! Working with them has been a pleasure, and I have been astonished at the gracious kindness, thoughtfulness and care they have always shown me as we wrestled with questions of clarity, accuracy and presentation. They have been brilliant, too, at chasing quotations.

Finally, I want to thank my wife, Diana. She has frequently mopped my fevered brow. But, far more than that, she has read every draft of this book, and made detailed notes full of corrections and possible improvements. In gratitude to her, I would like to quote, slightly adapted, the words of the first-century sage, Johanan ben Zakkai: 'If all the heavens were parchment, and all the trees were pens, and all the seas were ink, that would not be enough for me to record' the help, inspiration and encouragement that Diana has been to me during the last fifty-seven years.

*John Collins*
*Oxford*
*12.12.12*

## *What is this diagram?*

The yellow line fixes our attention on five great events that took place in Jesus Christ's days on earth and shortly afterwards.

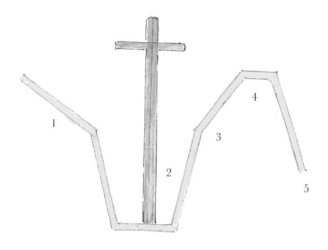

Event 1: Jesus died
Event 2: Jesus died and was buried
Event 3: Jesus was raised
Event 4: Jesus ascended
Event 5: Jesus poured out the Holy Spirit

I love the empty cross because it reminds me that God has raised Jesus from the dead, and that Jesus is alive forever. But what I took far too long to discover was that, linked to the death and resurrection of Jesus, are five spiritual blessings. There is a fairy-story quality about these spiritual blessings. They are astonishing. We would never guess them in a million years. If we come to understand them, we discover that these five spiritual blessings are life-transforming. They fulfil our wildest dreams.

The aim of this book is to make sure that we find them, and that we are helped to *share* them with our friends.

## *Notes*

1. Taken from the hymn, 'Amazing Grace'.

2. Spotted by Warnie, brother of C. S. Lewis, and mentioned in Walter Hooper (ed.), *C. S. Lewis: Collected Letters*, Vol. III (HarperCollins, 2006).

3. Keep It Simple, Stupid.

*Chapter 1*

# Jesus Died

Computer icons do remarkable things. Nudge one with your mouse and, in the twinkling of an eye, long columns rearrange themselves in alphabetical order or according to date. Nudge another and, in a flash, a paragraph with rumpled edges becomes shipshape – like this page, in which the ends of each line are perfectly aligned with the margin. A label then appears. On it is the word 'justify'.

Now for thousands of years, the word *justify* has meant something entirely different. So when we meet it in the New Testament, we must say goodbye to mice, menus, megabytes, and the other gobbledegook of the computer. *Justify* is a legal term. We need to think of the law courts, and words that a judge uses when he is sitting on the bench.

Perhaps you think, 'This is clearly a technical term. Is it really necessary for me to grapple with it?' No, it is not. But only by wrestling with the word *justify* can we understand some of the most staggering statements in the Bible. Indeed, in Christianity, to be justified is so unspeakably wonderful and so surprising that, at first sight, we may feel that God is playing some sort of game with us. Of course God is doing nothing of the kind. It is just that our feelings are at odds with what God says. It is like our experience of the universe. Sitting in the garden, we *feel* that we are stationary, whereas in reality we are hurtling through space at 66,600 mph.

Let me try to whet your appetite a little more by quoting two words of St Paul. The first is *peace*, peace with God. The second is *access*, access into God's presence. Isn't this exactly what we want? Paul links both with being justified.

Opposite one of the homes where we lived was a gaunt town pub. It was a grim building, with no brightly painted sign, and no roses up the front. Here, late one Saturday night, came a certain Mr Nicholson to refresh himself. He was a tall man, immensely strong, well-known to the police, and with a reputation for cruelty to his wife and children. By half-past eleven, he had persuaded himself that I had run off with his wife. So he came across the road to reclaim her. As he walked up the short drive, he picked up a lump of granite.

Happily, that particular vicarage, built in 1876, was designed to withstand a siege. There was a massive outer front door, studded with square iron nails. This had been shut and bolted. However, Mr Nicholson began to throw his lump of rock repeatedly at this outer door. The noise was ear-splitting. We all woke up. Had the third world war broken out? The three men who lived in the house gathered in the hall, armed with brooms and with a weighty ebony bust of a long-eared Maasai warrior, with which to tap Mr Nicholson's balding head – should it become a possible target. However, my wife, Diana, was the heroine of the evening. The bathroom being above the front door, she steadily poured jugfuls of water over him. He said in court, two days later, that he remembered that there was heavy rain at the time.

It was a near thing. He broke down the outer door, and the glass of the inner door. But I fulfilled a lifetime ambition. I rang 999. The police arrived. He was taken away.

I wish that I could tell you that Mr Nicholson had come to see me the following week and that he had said, 'I'm really sorry, Rev, that I gave you, and your mates, a bad night. But, I wasn't really responsible for my actions – y'see.' If he had done, I would have put out my hand, (wouldn't you?) and said, 'That's a generous apology, Mr Nicholson. I accept it, fully. In future let's be friends. Let's be *at peace* with each other.' But, of course, I could have gone further. I could have said, 'Now that we're friends, my wife and I would like you to regard this as your second home. When you pass down the road, come in. The front door is always open to you.' That would have been *access*.

It is precisely these two privileges, amongst countless other blessings, that God gives us once we are justified. 'We have *peace* with him.' No longer are we on the run, afraid to face him. He is on our side. He is our friend forever, and we know it. More than that, we have *access* to him. Access is the privilege of children. Children don't ring the bell; they run in and out of the home: in and out, all day.

So what does it mean to be justified? And how does it bring about peace with God?

It means something like this. The setting is a court of law. If we think of the Law Courts in Fleet Street, we will get the idea. But this is the heavenly court. God is the Judge. He has taken his seat. We are in the dock.

We are apprehensive, even frightened, and with good reason. We know enough about God's laws to feel guilty. We know, too, that Jesus, who is pure love, had spoken of destruction as a possible penalty. As children, we may have read *The Pilgrim's Progress* in which the author, John Bunyan, depicted Christian, the hero of the story, as a man born in the City of Destruction, clutching a piece of parchment on which was written, 'Fly from the wrath to come.' Was there any truth in this? If so, why had our family, and most of our friends, never taken the warning seriously?

Let me make the court scene even more personal. *I* am standing in the dock. This is what happens.

God looks at me. At length he speaks. 'John Collins, I know *all* about you. I know *everything* you have done in your life – every word, every deed. I have listened to all your thoughts, all your fantasies. Some of these words, acts and thoughts are such that I would prefer not to share them with other members of the court. I will spare you the embarrassment. Nonetheless, because you have pleaded guilty and put your trust in my Son, Jesus Christ, and because of what he did for you on the cross, and *only for that reason*, I declare … .' Here there is a long pause while I fear the worst … .

Then God continues, with a smile:'… that you are *absolutely righteous* in my sight.'

Isn't that astonishing? Did I hear rightly? Indeed, it is so wonderful that I can scarcely believe it. God loves us so much, says St Paul, that he 'justifies the wicked'.[1] I laugh with joy as I run down the steps outside the heavenly court, astounded by the goodness and kindness of God. Acquitted! Not guilty! Forgiven! At last, through Christ, I can stand tall in the presence of God.

Now put yourself in my place. Do you believe this – for yourself?

Perhaps you say, 'Of course I *want* to believe it. Who wouldn't? But this sounds a bit too good to be true; like lottery winners … . On Monday, they are too poor to buy a sandwich: by Tuesday, they have scooped up £20,000,000. "I can't believe it," they say. "Nah, it's impossible. I'm dreaming." So it is with new Christians. On Monday they are broke, spiritually. On

Tuesday, they are "heirs of God". They can't believe it – for joy. "I'm dreaming," they say.'

Well, it *is* very strange. Guilty men and women stand before a judge, and the judge proceeds to do exactly what judges must *never* do – acquit the guilty. And St Paul is not talking about a human judge. He is talking about God. How can God do such a thing?

## Event 1: Jesus died

The guilt and punishment of sin is taken away for those who put their trust in him.

Sin

God's judgment

The human race

**Jesus:** The head and representative of the human race

In the diagram, the human race is *under* the power of sin, and, therefore, *under* the judgment of God.

How can we be forgiven?

*'Look, the Lamb of God who takes away the sin of the world.'*
John 1:29

I am sure that you know the answer already – at least partly – or you would not be reading this book. The key phrase in the Judge's statement was 'because of what he (Jesus) did *for* you on the cross'. Whether or not we realised it, the most important milestone in our Christian pilgrimage was when we looked at the cross and saw that Christ was doing something there, not just for the world, but for us. More than that, he was doing something for *me*. 'He was pierced for *my* transgressions, he was crushed for *my* iniquities',[2] and he was bearing the punishment and guilt of *my* sins. He was dying in *my* place. When we grasp this, at last we can say with St Paul, Jesus 'who loved me and gave himself for me'.[3]

In 1917, during the First World War, the Prince of Wales (later King Edward VIII) was visiting a military hospital at Hanwell in Middlesex. The matron took him through the wards, one by one. At the end of the tour the prince said, 'I was told that there were nine wards in the hospital, and you have only taken me to eight.' The matron blushed, and replied, 'That is very observant of you, Sir. There is, in fact, one more room; but the soldier there is so hideously wounded that we wanted to spare you.' Edward insisted on seeing him. Most of the man's face had been blown off. The prince was silent for a few minutes. Then he knelt by the bed, and whispered, 'Thank you ... Oh, thank you ... for being wounded for me.'

When we kneel before another Man, dying on a cross, and we whisper, 'Thank you ... Oh, thank you for being wounded for me,' that is the decisive moment.

Immediately, God does two things. First, he forgives us. Jeremiah expressed it perfectly when he said that God would 'remember [our] sins no more.'[4] Think for a moment what that means. One day we shall see Jesus 'face to face'. Overwhelmed by the beauty of his holiness, we may well stutter, 'Oh Lord, I am *so*, *so* sorry that I did that dreadful thing in 1989 ... and said that hurtful thing in 2002.' Jeremiah tells us that heaven's forgiveness is so perfect that the Lord will look at us with a puzzled smile and say, 'Did you? I really don't remember.' God has the will to forget.

But second – and this is the extraordinary thing – God doesn't stop at forgiveness. He does something even more astonishing. By an act, like the touch of a royal sword on the shoulder, he changes our relationship with himself forever. He justifies us.

# *We are still poring over Event 1: Jesus died*

Christ died for me and I am justified.

The devil
Sin
Adam[5]

The human race

**Jesus**, the last Adam

*'To the man who
… trusts God who
justifies the wicked,
his faith is credited as
righteousness.'*
Romans 4:5

*'Therefore, since we have been justified through
faith, we have peace with God through our Lord
Jesus Christ.'*
Romans 5:1

This is a signal honour. It is one thing to be a forgiven sinner or a pardoned criminal. As such, while we are here on this earth, we are rightly humbled by memories of the past. It is quite another thing to be declared a righteous person. And that, apparently, is how God views us. That is how he treats us. That is how he always wants us to think of ourselves.

So, to our delight, we discover that this ancient word to 'justify', or to 'declare righteous', is the gateway that can bring us into God's presence with a song, and can keep us there throughout our lives in the sunshine of his love.

Now a step further. St Paul's teaching on being declared righteous by grace and faith was not new. It was foreshadowed in the Old Testament;[6] and years later, Jesus, with incomparable artistry, made it an important point in one of his parables.[7] In the story of a whimsical wedding, he hinted, in veiled language, that God actually *gives away* HIS righteousness. You see it's the same idea as 'declaring righteous', but decked out differently. The setting is now a wedding party instead of a court of law.

Here is the story in my own words.

'This was no ordinary wedding. It was a *royal* wedding. The cake was five feet high,[8] and contained twenty-four bottles of rum. It was a great occasion. The invitations went out early. You would assume that all the king's subjects would have given their eye teeth to be there.'

Then comes the first odd twist in the story. 'The guests, with extraordinary rudeness, didn't bother to come. The king realised that some sort of rebellion was afoot. Nevertheless he was determined that his generosity should not be wasted. So he ordered his servants to go out into the streets and hedges and to bring in the poor, the lame and the blind. They, at least, would appreciate his kindness. And they did. Instead of the great and the good, there arrived at the palace a dirty, ragged, disreputable but happy crowd. They had nothing to do, except to have a wash and to put on simple white linen wedding clothes, and they looked superb. Imagine the conversation. "Fancy meeting you here, Bill! And there's old Bert. Used to sleep under a hedge. Scarcely knew him in all that finery." They were ready to join the party and to meet the king. They couldn't believe their luck.'

Now comes the second odd twist; and, with this, the story reached its climax. 'The king, moving round in the crowd, talking, laughing, and enjoying his guests, suddenly came face to face with a guest who was not properly dressed for a wedding. Naturally, he was hurt and angry, and he called for his bouncers. The guest was thrown out.'

For many years, I was puzzled. I had an uncomfortable feeling that the poor man had been harshly treated. Perhaps he could not afford wedding clothes. Why then should he be cast into 'outer darkness'? St Augustine came to my rescue. In the ancient world, he explained, *the host* was responsible for providing appropriate clothing, not only for himself, but for the *whole* party. This was a long robe of white linen, handed out at the door when the guests arrived. So this guest, who had slipped into the reception in his dirty old jeans, had no excuse. He knew what he was doing. He was not only being rude; he was being deliberately presumptuous. He was making a point. 'I don't need special clothes to meet the king. I'm all right as I am.'

'The story ends with the king and his guests enjoying a marvellous party. And, perhaps for the first time, the guests realised what an amazingly good and generous king he was. All except one; and he got what he deserved.'

We can see that this story was a brilliant illustration of the doctrine that God, in Christ, was providing what he himself demanded. God gave Jesus, the perfect man, the task of weaving a white linen robe every minute of his life. Each time he carried out the Father's will, each time he spoke the Father's words, each time he did the Father's works, more stitches were added. And when, on the cross, he cried out 'Finished!' the beautiful white linen wedding clothes were ready. In future, they would be offered, free, to anybody who wanted to put them on. So this sort of righteousness is a gift of God. It is perfect. It comes from God. It is utterly unlike our own feeble attempts to be good, whether religious or otherwise. Nothing *we do* will ever bring it to us. Yet, it is very near us – only a prayer away – the prayer in which we put our *trust* in Jesus, make him our Lord and Saviour, and become one in him. In God's glorious plan, we are justified by faith or not at all. There is no other way.

There is something else that needs to be said. Earlier, I mentioned in passing the 'wrath' of God. The words cry out for explanation. They mean God's settled hatred of sin and evil, and his determination that, one day, he will judge and punish it. 'If I did not believe that all the evils and injustices of life throughout history were going to be made right by God in the next life', said Cardinal Newman, 'why, I think I would go mad.' How right that was. What of Huguenot fugitives all chained in galleys for the rest of their lives? What of the millions who died slowly in the gulags of Siberia? What of the noble army of Christian martyrs, ignored by the media, who have given up their lives in the last fifty years – a far larger number worldwide than in any age of church history? What of the violence, wickedness and misery that is reported night after night on the television? Indeed, there will be a future day of judgment. Jesus came and died so that we might escape that awful day. But it remains very real. Hence the warning, 'Fly from the wrath to come.'

Also, a word of warning to avoid a mischievous error. No illustration is perfect, and the story about the judge in the courtroom, or the story about King Edward VIII visiting Hanwell hospital, might seem to suggest that

God (one person) punished a compassionate Christ (a second person), because of my guilt (a third person). But that is a parody of the doctrine. Rather, '*God*' says St Paul, 'was *in* Christ, reconciling the world to himself'.[9] This was God's loving purpose for us from before the Big Bang.

At the cross, in John Stott's magnificent phrase, we see 'the *self*-substitution of *God*'. There are always mysteries, which we can never penetrate, in the doctrine of the Trinity. They come to a climax at the cross in those hidden hours of darkness that engulfed Jesus there.

So, once again, we return to our original question. How is it possible for God to say, 'I declare you righteous'?[10] The answer to this question is so important that I want you to consider one more way, a third way, in which it has been put.

As we've seen, undoubtedly there will be a *future* day when God will judge the world. Thankfully, that day has not yet dawned and, in the meantime, God says kindly to us, 'If you would like it, and if you are prepared to make Jesus your Saviour, *I will bring your case forward.*' Of course we are found guilty. But the punishment falls, not on *us* who deserve it, but on *Jesus*. Here are his own words: 'Truly, truly I say to you, he who hears my word and believes him who sent me, *has* eternal life; he does not come into judgment,' (Why not? Can you give the answer?) 'but has passed from death to life.'[11] So, notice something else in Christianity that you would never guess in a thousand years. In Islam, and in other religions, the judgment day comes *at the end* of life. That is what we would expect. Indeed that is what most people imagine – if they think about it at all. But Christianity is full of surprises. For the Christian, the judgment comes *at the beginning* of the Christian life. Thus a Christian need never be haunted by the fear of old sins being brought to light. They never will be. They have been judged and punished already.

Upon a life I did not live, [that is,
the righteousness of Jesus wrapped round me
– the wedding clothes of the story];
Upon a death I did not die, [that is,
Jesus took my place and was 'wounded for me'];
Another's life, another's death,
I stake my whole eternity.[12]

When we bring together 'another's life and another's death', as this hymn does, we can begin to see why the unknown author of the second-century *Letter to Diognetus* became so excited over what he called 'The Sweet Exchange'. 'O sweet exchange,' he wrote, 'benefits surpassing all expectation: that the wickedness of many should be hid in a single righteous One, and the righteousness of One should justify many transgressors.' Never was this glorious doctrine seen more clearly than in the seventeenth century. Theologians pounced on it, and renamed it 'The Great Exchange'. The Great

Exchange, they said, takes place, all five lines of it, in the twinkling of an eye, when we put our *trust* in Christ. Here it is in today's language. Those older thinkers would want us to read slowly, asking after each line 'Have I entered into this blessing that Christ has won for me?'

At the cross:

Christ takes my sins: he declares me righteous.

He takes my guilt: he gives me forgiveness.

He takes my curse:[13] he gives me his blessing.

He takes my shame – memories I dare not face: he gives me his glory.

He takes my rejection:[14] he gives me his love.

When God says, 'I declare that you are absolutely righteous in my sight,' a new relationship with him begins. It is a perfect relationship. It won't grow more perfect as we become better Christians. It won't be more perfect in heaven. Indeed, it is the one perfect relationship in the world. *At once* (because the barrier of sin has gone), the Holy Spirit of Jesus invades our lives. He quickly makes his presence felt. We, too, want to be holy. We want to be like Jesus.

For that reason, these two, being justified on the one hand, and becoming more holy – more like Jesus – on the other hand, are *always* found together. They are like the heavenly twins, Castor and Pollux, in the night sky. If you find one, you will find the other. They rub shoulders. Nevertheless, it is important to keep 'being justified' and 'holiness' distinct in our thinking. *To justify* means *to declare* righteous: growing in holiness is *becoming* righteous. The *justifying* sort of *righteousness* has *no* degrees: holiness has *countless* degrees. *Justifying righteousness* is a gift of God, complete and eternal: holiness is a long process – like climbing a mountain. Some Christian climbers are near the bottom; others halfway up. And, when we think smugly that we are nearing the summit, lo and behold, another snowy peak rises into view.[15]

So, to return to the stars, we must never confuse the heavenly twins, being justified and growing in holiness. Always keep some dark blue sky between them.

To sum up: when God declares us righteous in his sight, we are like dark hills, suddenly 'robed in a garment of untrodden snow.'[16] I therefore return to my original question, 'Do we believe this *for ourselves*?'

Here is a test: it is assumed that we *are* trusting in Christ. How righteous do we think we appear in God's sight? As righteous as St Paul? As righteous as Mother Teresa? As righteous as Janani Luwum, Archbishop of Uganda and martyr? As righteous as St Francis of Assisi? As righteous as Jesus Christ?

What do you think?

## *Believing pages*

The astounding answer, almost too good to be true, is, of course, Jesus Christ. His righteousness is wrapped round us like a cloak.

> *'He [God] justifies the one who has faith in Jesus.'*
> Romans 3:26, NRSV

Do you believe this – for yourself?

What are the immediate consequences?

> *'Therefore, since we have been justified through faith, we have peace with God through our Lord Jesus Christ, through whom we have gained access … .'*
> Romans 5:1–2, NRSV

A hymn[17] puts it like this:

> *So near, so very near to God,*
> *I cannot nearer be;*
> *Yet in the person of his Son*
> *I am as near as he.*
>
> *So dear, so very dear to God,*
> *More dear I cannot be;*

*The love wherewith he loves the Son:*
*Such is his love to me!*

Do you believe this − for yourself?

Then express your faith in love and praise.

A prayer to pray − very slowly, line by line:

*Heavenly Father, I am amazed at your love.*
*Thank you that Jesus died for me on the cross.*
*I rest, not in anything I have done,*
*but totally on him.*
*And so I trust what you say about me.*
*I believe that you declare me absolutely*
*righteous in your sight.*
*Thank you, oh, thank you.*
*And I praise you and bless you for*
*what you have given to me*
*In Jesus Christ, my dear Lord and Saviour, Amen.*

# *Notes*

1. Romans 4:5.

2. Isaiah 53:5–6, NIV, adapted.

3. Galatians 2:20, NRSV.

4. Jeremiah 31:34.

5. The mention of Adam may seem quaint, but in the Old Testament, Adam is the head and representative of the human race, which suffered greatly from his disobedience. In the New Testament, Jesus is the head and representative of a new race – those who put their trust in him, who are hugely blessed through his obedience. He is therefore called 'the last Adam'. Be patient! We shall say more about this in Chapter 2.

6. Isaiah 61:10; Isaiah 53:11.

7. Matthew 22:1–14. See also Luke 18:14.

8. The height of the cake at the wedding of Prince Philip and Queen Elizabeth II.

9. 2 Corinthians 5:19, NKJV (my italics).

10. The word 'justify' is only one of a number of words that New Testament writers use to explain the cross, but it is the foundation on which the others are built. For a full treatment, I strongly recommend J. R. W. Stott, *The Cross of Christ* (IVP, 1986).

11. John 5:24, RSV (my emphasis).

12. Horatius Bonar, 'Christ for us', *Communion Hymns* (1881).

13. The curse on those who break God's laws (Galatians 3:10).

14. I think of a husband whose wife deserted him for another man. He said to me, 'I wouldn't wish this on my worst enemy.'

15. Jesus warned us against becoming spiritually too big for our boots – imagining that we had achieved perfection, or anything like it. See Luke 17:10: 'When you have done *everything* you were told to do [you] should say, "we are unworthy servants; we have only done our duty." '. However, I suspect that he said this with a smile.

16. Percy Bysshe Shelley (1792–1822), from 'Queen Mab'.

17. From 'A Mind at Perfect Peace', attributed to Horatio Bonar.

*Chapter 2*

# Jesus Died and Was Buried

We have now reached Event 2 in the diagram. A prayer we Christians pray frequently is 'Lead us not into temptation, but deliver us from evil' (or more accurately) from the evil one.[1] So a good question to ask is this: To what extent do I actually experience this deliverance? Do I win?

In 1900 a young missionary named John Hyde sailed to India. A few days after his arrival, he went to a meeting where an Indian Christian spoke first about freedom from the guilt of sin and then about freedom from the power of sin. John listened carefully. At the end of the talk, somebody in the audience asked a question: How had this worked out in the life of the speaker? Could *he* say that Jesus had delivered *him* from the power of sin? There was a long silence. Then the Indian replied, 'Of course it is utterly through the grace of God; but I must answer, "Yes". I can

35

say, humbly, that I have been set free.' John thought to himself, 'If I had been answering that question, I would have had to say "No" – or be dishonest.' He was profoundly disturbed. He went back to his room, fell on his knees and prayed, 'Lord, unless you deal with the sins in my life, I might as well go home to England. I shall be no use here.'

God heard that prayer. During the following weeks John studied Romans chapter 6, and discovered how he, too, could experience freedom from the power of sin. From then on God used him mightily. John Hyde was not impressive to look at; he was slow of speech, and slightly deaf. Yet he held crowds spellbound. He became known and loved as 'Praying Hyde'.

Before I go any further, let me make one thing as clear as I possibly can. In Romans chapter 6, St Paul is not writing about freedom from the *presence* of sin. He is writing about freedom from the *power* or the *reign* of sin. In this world we shall always have to fight temptation. And fighting is well worthwhile – if we win. On the other hand, we ought to be deeply concerned if habits or patterns of sin continue long into the Christian life; if we continually moan and groan over our failures; if we say, 'I wish I could give up … but I can't. I struggle, but I fail again and again. I long to be free, but I'm not. I'm like a bluebottle climbing up a windowpane on a hot summer's day. Slowly, slowly up it goes; then with a frustrated buzz down it falls; again and again.'

The problems vary widely. Cries for freedom from irritability, freedom from the love of money, freedom from the need of recognition, freedom from greed, freedom from sexual sin, freedom from indulging in unkind criticism, freedom from laziness, freedom from the inability to forgive: all these cries are common enough.

There is an African parable that goes like this. A man was walking through the forest and came upon a baby monkey. He played with it for a few minutes and found it such delightful company that he decided to take it with him on his journey. The monkey had two particularly endearing habits. After play, it would climb up the man's back, sit on his neck, and snuggle affectionately against his head. And then, when the man was eating, the monkey would stretch out a paw and take some of the meat, half the banana, and most of the mango. So for many days they travelled happily through the forest.

The monkey grew rapidly, and the man found it heavy. But they stayed together because the man was lonely, and he loved the monkey's company.

At length, one morning, they had an especially good breakfast; at least, the monkey did. When they had finished, the man tried to get up. But he found he couldn't move. The monkey was too heavy. Eventually he struggled to his feet and took a few stumbling steps along the path. Fear gripped his heart. In desperation he shouted, 'Get off my back!'

The monkey, now completely in control, looked down at him balefully.

'Drop dead!' it said.

And the man dropped dead.

Do we understand the parable? Do we identify with it?[2] If so, we may well cry out, 'Oh ! ... but how? How can this *power* of sin be mastered?' The secret (happily an open secret) lies in the answer to two questions raised by Romans chapter 6.

## *Event 2: Jesus was buried*

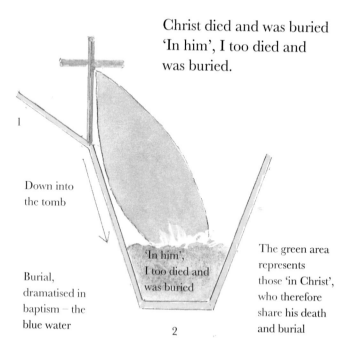

Christ died and was buried
'In him', I too died and
was buried.

1

Down into
the tomb

Burial,
dramatised in
baptism – the
blue water

'In him',
I too died and
was buried

2

The green area
represents
those 'in Christ',
who therefore
share his death
and burial

*'Don't you know that all of us who were baptised into Christ Jesus were baptised into his death? We were therefore buried with him through baptism into death ....'*
Romans 6:3–4

*'We know that our old self was crucified with him ....'*
Romans 6:6

*'I have been crucified with Christ ....'*
Galatians 2:20

The first question is this. What do we see when we look at the cross?

You say, 'I see Christ crucified for me.' Yes, indeed; but is that *all* you see? Clearly St Paul saw more. Of course, he saw Jesus dying for him. But he saw *himself* there, too. He writes, 'We know that our old self (that is, all that we were before we became Christians) *was crucified with him,*' and he is so anxious that we should grasp what he is writing that he repeats it five times in verses two to seven. 'We died ...' (verse 2) '... into his death' (3). 'We were buried with him ... into death' (4) '... united with him ... in his death ... ' (5). '... was crucified' (6). '... anyone who has died' (7). He writes the same in his letter to the Galatians: 'I am crucified with Christ, nevertheless I live ... ' (2:20, KJV). Somehow he sees his 'I' there: on the cross with Jesus. But what does this mean? Clearly none of us has actually undergone this fearful death. I have no scars in my hands and feet, nor have you; and nor had St Paul.

The explanation lies in the glorious doctrine of our union with Christ. From our first step of faith, however wobbly, God sees us as joined to him. We really are! Paul is startled that the Christians in Rome had not grasped this truth. 'Don't you know ...?' he asked in amazement. We are like sugar in a cup of tea: indeed, joined so perfectly that we become part of his body. And this is how God *always* now sees us. We are '*in* Christ'. This is a curious expression. After all, we may admire Winston Churchill or Albert Einstein. But however deeply we respect them, it would never occur to us to say, 'I am a man *in* Churchill, or 'I am a woman *in* Einstein'. Yet to be 'in Christ' is the way that Christians are described in St Paul's writings 164 times. We can only assume that the first Christians were determined that people should understand that a 'Christian' (a word used only three times in the New Testament) was somebody who shared a common life with the living, resurrected Lord. They were men or women *in him*, like, for instance, an eye or an ear *in* a body – only alive because that body was pumping blood into them; or a branch *in* a tree – only alive because of the sap rising from the trunk. Since the term 'Christian' now seems to mean little more than 'kind' and 'tolerant', a healthy step might be to return to this ancient usage and, when asked our religion on government forms, write 'I am a man in Christ', 'I am a woman in Christ'.

However, to pursue the main argument, do we now begin to see what St Paul is saying? There is a timelessness about the cross. He is stating, as forcibly as he can, that if we now share Christ's life, this implies that we have shared in his death, shared in his burial; and, as we shall come to see, shared in his resurrection and ascension. He is puzzled that the Christians at Rome have not grasped this. 'Don't you know?' he asks in astonishment.[3]

But we can go further. Paul's argument in Romans 6 begins in chapter 5, verse 14, where he suggests that, in the Bible, the two most influential men in the history of the world are Adam and 'the one who [is] to come' (RSV), namely Christ. You say, 'Christ, yes; but why Adam?' Because both are the head and representative of a race: Adam of the human race; Christ of the vast family of all those who, down the ages, have put their trust in God. Of the two, Christ is of course immeasurably greater, and it is a delight to see the way in which Paul contrasts Adam and Christ at the end of chapter 5 (verses 15, 17–19):

if many died through *one* man's [Adam's] sin,
... <u>much more</u> [has] the grace of ... that *one*
man Jesus Christ abounded for many ... If,
because of *one* man's sin, death reigned through

that *one* man, <u>much more</u> will those who receive the abundance of grace … reign … through the *one* man Jesus Christ … as *one* man's sin led to condemnation for all men, so one man's act of righteousness leads to acquittal and life for all … For as by *one* man's disobedience many were made sinners [ie we were all born on the pirate ship], so by *one* man's obedience many will be made righteous.[4]

Eight 'ones'! Why all this repetition? Because Paul is making an important point. Whether we like it or not, we are all bound up in the bundle of life either with the one man Adam (for ill) or with the one man Jesus (for blessing).

So it was through Adam, and through what Adam did, that many ills come to us. But notice the two 'much mores'. The blessings in Christ far outweigh the ills in Adam.

Being 'bound up in the bundle of life' is, I think, quite an easy idea to grasp. Josiah Guest owned an ironworks in South Wales. He was a good man with great ability. By 1830 his firm was producing 43 per cent of Britain's production of pig iron, and eventually provided railway lines for the UK, Russia and even China. In 1833 he sensibly married Charlotte, the gifted daughter of an earl, and they commissioned Sir Charles Barry, the architect of the House of Commons, to rebuild Canford Manor in Dorset. Alas, when they moved into their new home, they were not welcome. Why? Because Lady Charlotte had married 'into trade'. However, what might have been a sad tale ended well. Josiah and Charlotte held a grand dinner party. During dinner, Josiah arranged for the butler to bring him a note on a silver tray. The note announced the profits of the iron works for *one* year: £150,000 – many millions today. The figure leaked out, as Josiah intended. He and Charlotte were soon accepted in the highest social circles!

At length I come to my point. Josiah raised a large family, including two boys, Augustus and Montague. On the walls of the little Saxon church of Canford Magna there are memorial tablets to these children: one to Augustus, 'Master of Foxhounds for the Black Vale Hunt'; another to Montague, on which we are told that 'he died at Sandringham on a visit to his friend King Edward VII'. The place where Montague died did much to comfort the family in their loss.

## *Event 2 continued: Jesus was buried*

Adam, 'the first man', as St Paul calls him in 1 Corinthians 15:47, was head and representative of the human race. Jesus, the 'second man' is head and representative of a new race – the Christian family or the church.

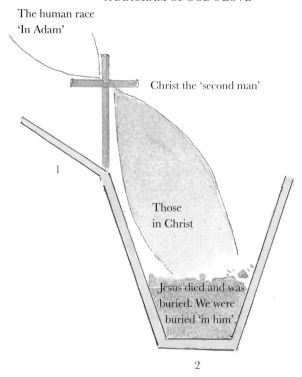

The human race
'In Adam'

Christ the 'second man'

1

Those
in Christ

Jesus died and was
buried. We were
buried 'in him'.

2

'As "in Adam" all die, so "in Christ" all will be
made alive.'
1 Corinthians 15:22

'The first man was ... dust of the earth; the
second man is of heaven.'
1 Corinthians 15:47

The point I am making is this. Augustus would not have been Master of Foxhounds,[5] and Montague would certainly not have died 'visiting his friend King Edward VII' if they had not been children of Josiah Guest. They were bound up in the bundle of life with their father. They *were what they were*, and they *did what they did* (very largely) because of the *one man* Josiah.

Less dramatically, the same is true for all of us. My grandparents were married in 1860. I have early photographs of them, looking bleakly out at the camera (clearly *not* dressed for Sandringham) and I think to myself, 'What odd-looking people.' But I can't escape. I am bound up in the bundle of life with them. What they *were*, and what they *did*, affects me today. So it is with Adam. And so it can be with Christ.

Thus, bringing Adam into the picture, which may well have struck you as quaint, turns out to be mysteriously up-to-date. Because Adam decided to be independent of God, 'in Adam' we inherited his 'rebellious gene'. In Christ we have a new family tree and we discover, to our joyful astonishment, that 'in Christ' we have inherited his 'I-want-to-please-God gene'.

About 100 years ago, there was a chaplain in the army named John Taylor-Smith. He loved to get groups of men together to talk to them about the Christian life and, in particular, about the cross of Christ. He would read to them the opening verses of Romans, chapter 6. Then he would say with a smile, 'When you look at the cross, what do you see?' They would say, 'Well, we see the three crosses, and the women standing at the foot of the cross ... and the centurion on his horse.' 'Yes, and what else do you see?' 'Well now ... Jesus on the central cross, and the two thieves on either side. Oh ... and Jerusalem in the background, and the black sky, and the soldiers gambling ... .' 'And what else?' Eventually, one of the men would say with a laugh, 'Come on, Sir. Put us out of our misery! What are you fishing for?' John Taylor-Smith would be silent for a moment, and then he would say – speaking very seriously – 'If that is *all* you see, then I suspect that you will be having trouble with your Christian life. You see, when I look at the cross, I see all that. But I see more. I see, nailed to the central cross, the old Taylor-Smith – all that I was before I became a Christian.'

We don't know quite how the conversation developed, but we can imagine Taylor-Smith continuing, 'I am not talking about anything *I* did. This was entirely the work of Christ. It was entirely what *he* did. He, as my representative, took me with him to the cross. When he was nailed to the cross – so was I (*in him*). When he died, I died (*in him*). When he was buried, I was buried (*with him*). When he rose to new life, I rose (*in him*). That is what St Paul is saying in Romans chapter 6. That is what I see when I look at the cross.'

Happily, we didn't remain in the grave. As we shall see when we come to Event 3 in the diagram, God raised Jesus from the dead; and in him we, too, are raised. In St Paul's words in Romans chapter 6, verse 4, 'We were buried ...', so that as Christ was raised from the dead 'by that splendid Revelation of the Father's power so we too might rise to life on a new plane altogether.'[6] Do you catch Paul's excitement? Even in the dull phrasing of the NIV 'may live a new life'? What is this 'new plane', this new life? Nothing less than a life set free from the *power* of sin.

## *Event 2 contd.: Jesus was buried*

> *'He has rescued us from the dominion of darkness and brought us into the kingdom of the Son he loves.'*
> Colossians 1:13

**The kingdom of darkness**     **The kingdom of Jesus**

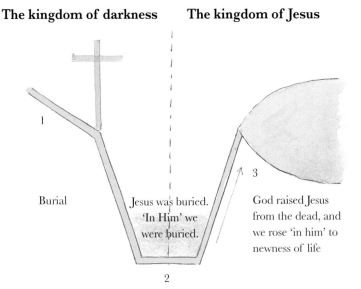

Burial

1

Jesus was buried.
'In Him' we
were buried.

2

3

God raised Jesus
from the dead, and
we rose 'in him' to
newness of life

Here I would ask you to look long and hard at the next diagram on p.49. This is probably the most important diagram in the book. Please notice the dotted line down the centre. Those on the left of that line are 'in Adam'. That is where at birth we all begin; and because of Adam's disastrous disobedience, we inherit his nature with its bias to sin; and ultimately, though we don't realise it, we are under the power of the devil.

However, for those 'in Christ' a momentous change has taken place. 'In him' we have been carried from one side of the diagram to the other side of the diagram. We have been 'rescued … from the dominion of darkness' (on the left) and 'brought … into the kingdom of the Son he loves' (on the right).[7]

We shall never go back. Now we are under God. Now we are under grace. Now we are free to serve Jesus with a new nature, 'as a new creation, in a new life, after a new way, with a new tongue and new manners, with new words and new works'.[8] We are on the right side of the page. That is how we are always to think of ourselves. For that, spiritually, is where we are.

## *Event 2 contd. Jesus was buried*

> *'He has delivered us from the dominion of darkness and transferred us to the kingdom of his beloved Son.'*
> Colossians 1:13, RSV

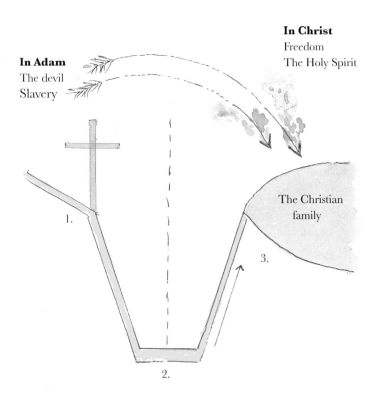

**In Christ**
Freedom
The Holy Spirit

**In Adam**
The devil
Slavery

The Christian
family

1.

3.

2.

*'Put on the full armour of God, so that you can
take your stand against the devil's schemes. For our
struggle is not against flesh and blood, but against
the rulers, against the authorities, against the
powers of this dark world and against the spiritual
forces of evil in the heavenly realms. Therefore put
on the full armour of God ... take up the shield
of faith, with which you can extinguish all the
flaming arrows of the evil one.'*
Ephesians 6:11–16

There is a second truth to be drawn from the dotted line, and I can't emphasise these two truths too strongly. Yes, 'in Christ' we have been rescued and set free. *But*, the dark powers can still launch their attacks on us from the other side of the divide – see the flaming arrows on p.49. They will continue to do so as long as we live. They never give up.

So we must always remember that we are vulnerable. The flesh is weak. We need to be strengthened by asking God, every day, to fill us with the Holy Spirit. The devil will attack us at irregular and surprising moments, and in surprising ways, and the body (according to one seventeenth-century theologian) is his 'landing-port'.[9]

So he tries to make us use some part of our body wrongly. And of course he hides. He hides behind the body. What do I mean? Well, a healthy appetite is one of God's splendid gifts. Yet, somewhere, there must be a boundary between a healthy appetite and gluttony. Is it between the first and second helping of chocolate pudding? Or between the second and third? Or between the third and fourth? Who can tell? We are not under law. But wherever our own particular boundary lies, the devil will try to push us over; and the thought he will drop into our mind will be, '*You have a healthy appetite*. You are free as a Christian. Why not? Have some more.' There are many timely answers to 'Why not?' Our weight, appearance, general health, our example as a Christian, and so on; above all, the will of the Lord. (Have we asked *him*?) The devil doesn't mention these. He hides. And we imagine that we are simply meeting the need of a healthy appetite.

Or the devil may hide behind our temperament. The Christian family presents an extraordinary jumble of different temperaments. That is what makes it so fascinating. Every temperament is needed, and God has a plan for each within the body of Christ. 'Wednesday's child is full of woe.' She fears the worst. The devil pushes her to be a grouser, a sour puss. 'You can't help it', he whispers. 'You were born like that.' (Which is quite true.) 'You have the right to ooze gloom.' (Which is not.) In Christ she can become a deeply imaginative and sympathetic friend, and the habit of praising God each day could so balance and control her temperament that few would guess that she was naturally an Eeyore.

And then the devil hides behind our friends. Jesus came to this world in order to die: and he died in order to save. When he told the twelve disciples about the crucifixion and resurrection, Peter, one of his closest friends, was horrified. 'God bless you, Master,' he said, 'Nothing like this must happen to you.' Peter meant this in the kindest possible way. Jesus *crucified*? He couldn't bear the thought. But in his spirit Jesus felt that there was more in this kindly remark than met the eye. Behind Peter was the devil – trying to turn him from his Father's will. So he speaks sharply, not to Peter (what good would that have been?), but to the devil behind Peter and speaking through Peter: 'Out of my way, Satan! You stand right in my path.'[10]

So, too, for ourselves: it is absolutely no good fighting my body, my temperament, my family, my friends, my employer, or anybody else, however disagreeable and difficult they may be. These are not the real enemy. The *real* enemy is Satan. His arrows come from outside, they are dangerous, and can cause horrible wounds. But they can be caught with the shield of faith. What is this shield? To dare to believe what God says about us, and from that platform of faith to resist him with all our might. To speak to him sternly, in Jesus' name, knowing our authority in Christ; and continuing to do so until the attack fades away. There is nothing passive about the fight of faith. We have a cunning and persistent enemy. But this is a fight we can win.

Charles Spurgeon, who preached to a crowd of 22,000 at the opening of the Great Exhibition in 1851, learnt this lesson as a young man. He wrote in his diary:

> I was brought up, as a child, with such care that
> I knew very little of foul or profane language,
> having scarcely ever heard a man swear. Yet
> … in my earliest Christian days … there came
> into my mind thoughts so evil that I clapped
> my hand to my mouth for fear I should … give
> utterance to them. Once I went to see my dear

old grandfather. I told him about my terrible experience … 'Grandfather, I am sure I cannot be a child of God, or else I should never have such evil thoughts as these.'

'Nonsense, Charles,' answered the good old man. 'It is just because you are a Christian that you are thus tempted. These blasphemies are no children of yours; they are the devil's brats, which he delights to lay at the door of a Christian. Don't you own them as yours; give them neither house-room nor heart-room.'[11]

So an important part of conquering temptation is, first, to know that you are 'in Christ', and then, upon this basis, to fight the enemy.

Such pure Victoriana may make us smile, but this extract from the diary exposes the subtlety with which the powers of darkness attack us. First, the devil stands behind us and drops an evil thought into our mind: he can do this because he has access to our thoughts. Then he moves round to face us, accusing us of the very thought that he has implanted. It is therefore important to realise that often we can't help our thoughts, and that the thought becomes sin only when we say 'Yes' to it. Momentary thoughts and wishes will knock on the door, but don't ask them in to supper. Or, in Luther's words, 'We can't prevent the storks flying over our head, but we can stop them nesting in our hair.' If we give any heart-room to his 'brats', the devil uses them to attack our faith. 'You can't be a child of God,' he whispers, 'if you think things like that.'[12]

Here I must add some words of warning. We are not saying that we are dead to the *influence* of sin. Nor are we suggesting instant holiness. Holiness, as we shall see in chapter 3, should continue to grow lifelong. But it *is* instant *deliverance*, like the deliverance of the Jews from the cruel grip of Egypt – a miraculous work of God. One day they were slaves; the next they were free.

Equally, this is not some form of 'second blessing' – some spiritual experience that *necessarily* comes later. It is 'in Christ'. And, as you may have noticed in Romans chapter 6, our death with Christ is closely associated with baptism, the proper place for which is at the *beginning* of the Christian life. 'Do you not know,' he wrote, 'that all of us who have been baptised into Christ [have been] baptised into his death?[13] We were buried therefore with him by baptism into death'. I have indicated this many times on the diagram with blue water. Nevertheless, the beginning of the Christian life is like a cut diamond – multifaceted, and sometimes we don't see all the facets. I certainly didn't, as you will discover in a few pages' time. But that was my fault: and my experience was therefore subnormal. I am sure that there are plenty of Christians who are delivered from the power of sin on the happy day when they first put their trust in Jesus.

Nor is it freedom from the *presence* of sin, as if we could say, 'I will never sin again.' It is not freedom from the temptation to sin. Much trouble is caused when we jump to such false conclusions. But it *is* freedom from the *reign* of sin. The Christian can always say, 'I need not sin now.' It is the fulfilment of the dream of the prophets – 'Praise be to the Lord … because he has come … to rescue us from the hand of our enemies, and to enable us to serve him without fear in holiness and righteousness before him all our days.'[14] Isn't that exactly what we long for?

We now come to the second question. The first one, as you will remember was, 'What do we see when we look at the cross?' Here is the second one.

What do we see when we look at ourselves?

St Paul's answer is dazzlingly clear. We should always see ourselves on the right side of the diagram, as 'alive to God', as 'slaves of righteousness' and as 'slaves of God'.[15] In contemporary language, we should always accept that we are now *radically and totally different.* 'If anyone is in Christ, the new creation has come', he wrote to his friends at Corinth. 'The old has gone, the new is here!'[16] Paul became so excited as he wrote those words that he left out all the verbs in the first sentence.

Christian people often say with a moan, 'If you knew what I'm really like … I'm so bad-tempered … I'm such a jealous person … I'm such a useless person … I have a team of wild horses inside me, out of control,' and so on and so forth. A fair reply to such comments would be a puzzled smile, followed by, 'Really? I thought that you were a Christian. I thought that the "the old you" had died with Christ, and that you were a new person in Christ.' The person then tends to backtrack rapidly. 'You see,' I might continue, 'we don't *have* to be like that. And God most certainly does not see us like that.' Then why should we always think of ourselves negatively? We don't mean to; but are we not denying what God has done for us?

So, with St Paul, we need to say continually, 'I have been crucified with Christ.' What I was in Adam has died and has been buried. We must always begin there.

In his book *I Was A Stranger*, General Sir John Hackett described how, during the Second World War, he hid with a Dutch family. He had been wounded in the battle of Arnheim. A brave Dutch doctor visited him secretly. The doctor spoke no English, but he had looked up the word 'body' and a few useful phrases in the dictionary. So each morning, his opening remarks were the same. 'G-o-o-o-d morning, Mr Hackett. How is your ... corpse?' That was good theology! As bedside manner, maybe it left something to be desired.

Although what we were in Adam has died in Christ, the devil is crafty. He will try to make us *feel* that what we were in Adam has *not* died. And in the early days, until our faith is strong, we may well be like a disabled soldier whose legs have been amputated and yet who *feels* twinges of pain where his legs used to be. How does the devil do it? In the same way that he tempts us. He drops a bad thought into our mind, and then he whispers, 'There you are, you see. What you were in Adam is alive and well. You haven't changed a bit.'

But this is a lie. In Christ, a great change has taken place. In him, we died. In him, the funeral of our old life is over; it's in the past. The wounded soldier, poor man, has to face sad truth when he lifts the sheet and sees the empty bed where his legs should be. Christians face the joyful truth when they look again at what God says about them: 'Don't you know that all of us who were baptised into Christ Jesus were baptised into his death? We were therefore buried with him … .'[17] Don't you know this?

But we must not stop there. Yes, 'I have been crucified with Christ', but now I live, 'and the life that I now live, I live by faith in the Son of God who loved me, and gave himself for me.' Equally we must dare to believe that, in Christ, we have been spiritually raised from the dead, and that we are new people with a new life to live. We must always begin with what God has done. Professor A. W. Tozer once put it like this:

> When we see ourselves in a new way, and
> dare to believe what God says about us, *then*
> our actions change. We think that we have to
> behave differently *first*. God says, 'No. I have
> made you different, and when you believe
> it, your actions will automatically begin to
> change.'[18]

I had been ordained twelve years before I discovered these exhilarating truths. On Sundays I would pour out my heart from the pulpit, telling others that Christ was a wonderful Saviour, and I really believed it. I never doubted for a moment that, by his grace, I was forgiven. But sometimes, as I walked home, I would say to myself, 'Why isn't he more of a Saviour to me?' I felt like the poor man with the monkey.

One day in January 1963, I planned to attend a meeting in London. I caught the train at Gillingham in Kent, where we were then living. Heavy snow was falling. The train crept along the line and eventually stopped outside Gravesend. Clearly I was never going to reach my destination. So I said to myself, 'What shall I do? How can I avoid a wasted day?' It occurred to me that it was high time that I tried to understand that obscure chapter, Romans 6. I lifted my heart in prayer, took out my pocket New Testament and began to read. The first words that struck me were 'set free from sin' in both verses 18 and 22. I thought to myself, 'That is just what I want.' Then I noticed the phrase in verses 3 and 16 'Don't you know …?' St Paul seemed to be drawing attention to some elementary matter; as if he were saying 'Don't you know how to boil an egg?' or 'Don't you know how to spell "tomato"?' This was both puzzling and humbling – a wounding touch. I remember saying to God, 'Lord, I am sorry, but I *don't* know. Please show me.'

A few minutes later I was struck by the emphasis on *death*. Death was mentioned six times in the first seven verses, particularly in verse 6 with its confident '*We know* that *we* have been crucified … .' The thought came to me, 'Is it possible that Christ took, "the man I once was", "my old self", "the man in Adam" that has caused me so much trouble … is it possible that he took "all that I was in Adam" to the cross with him, and I have never realised it?'

This was a fresh thought for me. If it were true, why had I never heard it before?

All the way home in the train, and for the next few days, whenever I had time I turned to Romans 6 and meditated upon those first eleven verses. When Friday came, I decided that I must make up my mind and act. So, hesitatingly, I knelt at my desk. I prayed, 'Lord, I don't altogether understand this, but I *believe* what you say about me. I *believe* that *I* – my former self that has caused me so much trouble – died with you on the cross, and was buried with you, and that I really am a new person. Amen.'

I rose to my feet. I felt nothing. I sat down at my desk and continued with my work. Suddenly – it was most remarkable – a flood of evil filled my mind, followed by the thought, 'You see, you've got it wrong. You are exactly the same as you were before, just as you have always been.' I cried out in deep distress, 'Lord, I can't have got it wrong.' Immediately some other words sprang to my mind, 'He is a liar, and the father of lies', and I recognised them at once. They were the words of Jesus describing the devil in John 8:34.

At last I began to see, with desolating clarity, what had been happening. The devil has access to our thoughts. If this were not so, Jesus himself could not have been tempted. These ugly imaginings and temptations were from the devil. I remembered the command of St James, 'Resist the devil, and he will flee'.[19] So under my breath, I told him sharply, 'Go! I have been crucified with Christ. I am a new man. Be gone – in Jesus' name!' The temptation faded. I was fascinated.

On that first day I discovered that I had to repeat the exercise described in the last paragraph many, many times; but when night fell, I was thrilled, for I had experienced a long day of temptation, and yet had won. How had I been set free? Was it *my* strong will? Was it *my* determination not to fall – *my* struggles, *my* efforts? Not a bit of it! It was entirely and utterly the grace of God through what Jesus had accomplished at the cross. As Karl Barth used to say, 'Grace had taken me by the throat.' All *I* had done was *to trust* what God said about me; namely that I, the old John Collins, 'my former self', the man who was a slave of greed, anger, lust, critical of others and so on, had been nailed to the cross with Jesus.

On Sunday night, I decided to preach on what I had discovered. There was an elderly member of the congregation named Fred in church that evening. He had retired from Chatham dockyard, and was well known in the parish as an exceptionally good man. 'Fred will always do you a good turn' is the way his neighbours spoke of him. On one occasion I remember visiting him, and found him sitting at the kitchen table, reading his Bible; it seemed perfectly natural. At the end of the service, I went to the porch. Fred, a man of few words, usually passed by with a quiet 'Goodnight, Vicar'. That evening, he stopped. 'May I have a word with you, Vicar?' he said. 'Yes, of course', I replied, pulling him closer to me. 'You preached something new tonight, Vicar. Why haven't you preached it before?' 'If you really want to know, Fred,' I said, 'it's because I only discovered it last week.' A warm smile spread over his old face. 'I thought so,' he went on, 'but I would like you to know, Vicar, that I discovered it when I was a boy of sixteen.'

Now a step further. Nobody doubts that Jesus *died* on the cross. If I were to ask you, 'Did two thieves die with Jesus?' you would reply at once, 'Yes, of course. Everybody believes that – just as we believe that the Battle of Hastings was fought in 1066. These are facts.'

St Paul wants us to see that the statement *we died with him* is equally a fact. We have nothing to do except (to use his own word) to *know* it, or, as we might say, to realise it. He then goes on to say 'You … must consider yourselves dead … .' Why? Because in Christ we died with him, entirely objectively, over 2,000 years ago.

Some people have thought that we were 'dead' as long as we 'considered' ourselves dead. In the Authorized Version of 1611 the word was 'reckon': 'Likewise reckon ye also yourselves to be dead indeed unto sin …' (Romans 6:11). I once asked a thoughtful friend how he interpreted the word. He replied, 'Well it's true as long as you reckon it's true.' This, as I am sure you see, turns the doctrine on its head, and implies that we are trying to believe something that isn't true. It also places all the emphasis on *my* 'reckoning'. It suggests that, if I cease to 'reckon' myself dead, nothing works. So, ultimately, it is all up to me.

St Paul is not saying anything of the sort. He is saying, 'If you are in Christ, you died when he died,' and the words 'considering' or 'counting' (NIV) or 'reckoning' simply mean believing what has happened. A fact is a fact. The word 'fact' comes from the Latin 'factum' – something that has been done. What has been done? In more theological language, the cross towers timelessly and eternally over the universe, and Christ, the last Adam, took the old humanity to the cross with him. That included you and me.

Watchman Nee wrote about this in his book, *The Normal Christian Life*. 'I "reckoned" (in the wrong way) from 1920 to 1927,' he said, 'and I could not understand why nothing happened.' Then one day, as he was praying, he suddenly saw his 'oneness' with Christ. He added, 'I saw that I was in him, and that when he died, I died. I was carried away with joy.'

Perhaps you say, 'I don't feel as if I had died,' or 'I don't feel dead.' As so often in the Christian life, this is not a matter of feelings. The apostle is describing something that *has* happened to us. This is something that God *has done* to us in Christ. The only question is, 'Do we dare to believe what God says? Against our feelings, against the whisperings of the devil, against our past experience, are we prepared to hold on to the truth of the word of God?'

So our freedom from the power and tyranny of sin was won by Christ on the cross. It becomes ours when we take our stand on his promises, and maintain our stand, however fiercely we are tested by the powers of darkness. Take courage. We can win. In the power of the Spirit, a Christian may always say, 'I need not sin now.'

I want to add a little more about the end of Romans, chapter 6. You may have noticed that the first part of the chapter is simply a description of what God, with amazing kindness and love, has done through the death, burial and resurrection of Christ. There is no exhortation. There is no appeal to *us* to do anything, except to *know* – 'Don't you know …?', and to *believe*, 'You also must consider yourselves dead to sin and alive unto God in Christ Jesus.' Of course! Because when Christ died, we died. When Christ was buried, we were buried. And when Christ was raised, we were raised with him.

Then, for the first time, in verse 13, there is an appeal, and I can scarcely find words to say how important it is: '[offer] yourselves to God as men who have been brought from death to life, and your members [the different parts of your body] to God as instruments of righteousness'.[20] Never does St Paul say, 'You have been set free to do anything you like.' Rather, we *have already made* our choice. We have chosen not to stay on the left side of the diagram and be a slave of sin, and ultimately of the devil, who would have paid us a salary of shame and death. And, in Christ, too, we *have already* made our choice. We have chosen to move to the right side of the diagram where we are free to become slaves of God with an excellent salary of holiness, plus a huge bonus – eternal life.[21]

By the way, have you ever heard of a slave being given a fat salary? But Love has come, and has transformed everything.

In short: the only freedom open to us in this life is slavery to Christ. If we dare to go up that road, we find, paradoxically, that it leads to *perfect* freedom.

Archbishop Bill Burnet was Archbishop of Cape Town towards the end of the last century. After he had been a bishop for fifteen years, he went one Sunday to take a church service. His address was on 'the love of God shed abroad in our hearts by the Holy Spirit'. After the service, he drove home and, feeling tired he poured himself a drink, sank into a chair, and began to read the Sunday newspapers. Suddenly and strangely, he felt that God was telling him to pray. With some reluctance, he dragged himself out of the chair, went to his chapel and knelt down. The thought came to him, 'Give me your body.' This made him smile. He was tall, rugged, dignified, and rather a bag of bones; not a Mr Atlas. However, he thought he would pray a prayer based on St Paul's suggestion in Romans 6:13 of how we should respond to Christ's love on the cross. Here (again) are the exact words, '[offer] yourselves to God, as those who have been brought from death to life; and offer the parts of your body to him as instruments of righteousness.' So he began, 'Lord, here is my brain, to think your thoughts. Here are my eyes, to see what you want me to see. Here are my lips, to speak what you want me to say'… and so on. When he reached his feet in the prayer, he said afterwards, 'I *experienced* what I had spoken about in the morning. The love of God was poured into my heart. I found myself flat on the floor of the chapel, and God said to me, "You are my son."'

In many different ways, this proved to be a turning point in Archbishop Burnet's life and ministry. In his home, hidden from the diocese, he said that he had been difficult to live with, even, at times, resentful and bitter. From then on the Holy Spirit became a well of water in him, springing up, refreshing, empowering. How this happens is the theme of another chapter.[22]

## *Believing pages*

Chapter 2 was a long one, and covered much ground. Throughout it, the Holy Spirit may have been speaking to you. You were the man with the monkey. You were the fly climbing up the window pane. If so, for a moment, you must forget the diagram, and I would say gently, 'You need to repent.'

> *So turn your eyes upon Jesus.*
> *He is a Saviour. He is here to set you free.*
> *Come to him. Confess your sins to him.*
> *Tell him how sorry you are.*
> *Ask him to forgive you.*
> *Believe that he has done so.*

Then:

1. There is something to know. 'Don't you know that all of us who were baptised into Christ Jesus were baptised into his death? We were therefore buried with him …' (Romans 6:3–4).

Do you know this? Do you know that you died with Christ, and were buried with him?

If so:

2. Will you believe it? And will you continue to do so against your previous experience, and

against your feelings? And (if need be) against what others say?

Above all:
3. Will you believe it, against the lies and whispers of the devil?

> 'Resist the devil, and he will flee ...'
> James 4:7

If you are saying, 'Yes, yes, yes', here is a prayer to pray. I suggest you read it through first. Then pray it; praying each line very slowly and thoughtfully:

> *Lord Jesus Christ, I am amazed at your love.*
> *I am so grateful that you have rescued me from the power of sin.*
> *I believe that you took me to the cross.*
> *I believe that in you I died, and in you I was buried.*
> *I believe that in you I was carried across the gulf into your kingdom.*
> *I believe that in you I have been brought from death to life.*
> *So, ransomed, healed, restored, forgiven, I worship you and sing your praises. Amen.*[23]

Because in Christ you died, and in Christ you have risen to a new plane of life, in loving gratitude to God for all that he has done, 'as those who are alive from the dead,' therefore,

4. Surrender yourselves (i) to a person – the Lord Jesus. 'Offer yourselves to God, as those who have been brought from death to life.' Not, 'I will follow you, but … .' There are no 'buts' here. It's once for all, like Christian marriage.

Surrender yourself (ii) for a purpose. 'And offer the parts of your body to him as instruments of righteousness' (Romans 6:13). That is, surrender your body to him, so that he can use you to get his work done in the world.

So, another prayer to pray – a prayer of surrender. Again I would suggest you read it first, and then pray it very slowly, line by line:

*Lord Jesus, in love and deepest gratitude, I now offer myself to you. I offer you my eyes, my thinking, my lips, my tongue, my ears, my hands, my feet. Take me, all that I am, all that I hope to be, and use me in your glorious service. Amen.*

# *Notes*

1. That is why in the diagram on p. 23, Adam, representing mankind, is 'under sin', and ultimately under the power of the devil.

2. Do we identify with the parable of the monkey? If so, no one is more delighted than I am. But perhaps we don't. Some Christians experience deliverance from the power of sin from the moment of their conversion; but, alas, not all.

3. In Acts 1:1, Luke tells his friend Theophilus that in his first book he had written of the things 'that Jesus *began* to do and to teach' on earth. In his second book he is going to tell the story of what Jesus *continued* to do and to teach: this time from heaven *in* and through his followers by the power of the Holy Spirit. Read Acts 5:12–16 to see what happened. Nor was it only the apostles. See Acts 6:8; 1 Corinthians 12.

4. From the RSV, but with 'sin' used instead of 'trespass'.

5. My wife, Diana, visited a woman in Canford, and invited her to church. The reply was a firm 'No'. She said that she had once been to a service, and had sat under a memorial to a man who was Master of Foxhounds. She felt that this was very wrong, and she would never go there again. (Vicars and their wives sometimes have a hard life.)

6. J. B. Phillips, *Letters to Young Churches: A Translation of the New Testament Epistles* (Geoffrey Bles, 1947). A good translation not influenced by the majesty of the Authorized Version of 1611.

7. Colossians 1:13.

8. Bishop Lewes Baily, *The Practice of Piety*, 1636, p.563.

9. William Gurnall, *The Christian in Compleat Armour or a Treatise on the Saints War against the Devil*, 1655.

10. Matthew 16:22ff; J. B. Phillips, *The Gospels in Modern English* (Geoffrey Bles, 1952).

11. As quoted in Daniel Panther (ed.), *The Essential Works of Charles Spurgeon* (Barbour Books, 2009), page number unknown.

12. This is why the devil is called 'the accuser of our brothers', Revelation 12:10.

13. ESV. I have written more fully about baptism in Chapter 7, especially on pp.152–53; 'The practice of using the catacombs for burial may have become established amongst the Jewish community in Rome. In which case, baptism by immersion would be a clear picture of burial.' H. J. Leon, *The Jews of Ancient Rome* (Jewish Publication Society of America, 1960), p.66.

14. Luke 1:68, 74–75.

15. Romans 6:11, 18, 22, NKJV.

16. 2 Corinthians 5:17.

17. Romans 6:2–4.

18. Source unknown.

19. James 4:7, NRSV.

20. Romans 6:13, RSV.

21. Romans 6:11; 6:21; 6:22–23.

22. Romans 5:5.

23. You may like to pray the prayer again, this time turning it into thanksgiving and praise. 'Thank you, Lord Jesus Christ for your amazing love. Thank you for rescuing me …' and so on.

*Chapter 3*

# Jesus Was Raised

The arm of the diagram now changes direction, moving sharply upward. On the first Easter morning God raised Jesus from the dead, and, need I say, attached to this towering miracle there is a blessing and experience that we should enjoy. In him we, too, are raised to '*newness* of life'. Once we are justified, the way is wide open for the Holy Spirit (the very life of God himself) to come and live in us. Nothing less than a new world opens up.

Sir David Attenborough, naturalist and agnostic, was asked on the radio whether he ever thought that there might possibly be 'a Divine Force' ultimately responsible for this astonishing universe. He paused for a moment; then he said, 'I have spent many months researching termites. They are fascinating. I have often poked a termite mound with my walking stick, and made a little window into their castle. There they are, myriads of them, busily going about their lives. I confess that I have sometimes wondered whether any termite has ever imagined that there might be a big world beyond. But they show no desire to adventure out of the mound. They are blind, you see.'

Blindness is not only a termite problem. Jesus said that, in one way and in a very important way, we all begin life like termites. We *are* blind, not physically, but *spiritually*. Looking back, I can scarcely believe how blind I was – in God's sight a spiritual beggar, gazing blankly and pathetically upward, eyes rheumy and fly-ridden. Apart from the mercy of God, I, like the termites, would have spent a frenetic life on this little planet, going nowhere, totally unaware that all around me was the big heavenly world, the eternal world – far more glorious and spacious than this one, just as our present world is far more glorious and spacious than a termite mound.

This is true, even of religious people. Nicodemus was a distinguished teacher of the Jewish religion. In this country he would have been a regular churchgoer, a leading cleric, perhaps a bishop or a cardinal. Yet when he tried to joust with Jesus in a theological debate, Jesus went straight to the point. 'Nicodemus,' he said kindly, 'you must be born from above. Unless you are born from above, you will never even *see* the kingdom of God.'[1] How, with all that knowledge and all that expertise, could Nicodemus not *see* the kingdom? We know the sad answer. Like the termites, he was blind. Only the Holy Spirit could open his eyes.

Another description of God's family is 'the body of Christ'. Paul dignifies the Christians at Corinth, bad though some of them were, by telling them, 'You *are* the body of Christ' (1 Corinthians 12:27), not, 'You are *like* the body', but 'You are …'. Did he glimpse this on the road to Damascus when the Lord said to him, 'Why do you persecute *me*?' So each of us is part of Christ's body – an eye, a toe, a thumb. Some parts seem to be more important than others; but all are needed, including those that nobody knows about – like the spleen. We should give special honour to Christians who do good by stealth – quiet, hidden work for God that is easily overlooked.

## An Ode to the Spleen

Spare a thought for the hard-working spleen,
Although few of us know what it's for,
But it battles, unseen, to keep your blood clean,
Fighting toxins that come through the door.

It's a spongy and vascular organ
That filters out harmful bacteria,
Obsolete cells, foreign bodies as well.
To give us a spotless interior.

So next time you're venting your spleen
When you're angry, or feeling frustrated
Remember your spleen is working off-screen
To remove the bad blood that's created.[2]

But once our eyes are open and sparkling, what should we focus on? If God has transferred us out of one country (a dark one) into his own kingdom of light; or, remembering the diagram, if God has carried us from the left of the page, across the gulf, to the right – what should we look at first? Are there people we should get to know? Indeed there are.

## *Event 3: Jesus was raised*

Those who put their trust in him are raised to a new life in God's family.

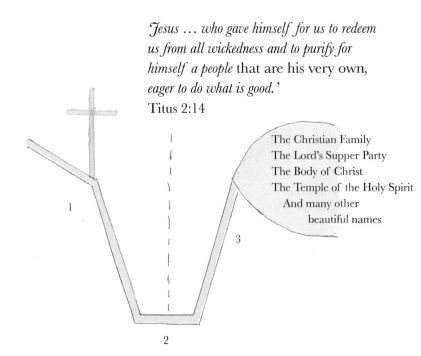

*'Jesus … who gave himself for us to redeem us from all wickedness and to purify for himself a people* that are his very own, *eager to do what is good.'*
Titus 2:14

The Christian Family
The Lord's Supper Party
The Body of Christ
The Temple of the Holy Spirit
And many other
beautiful names

1

3

2

It is important for our spiritual health to know that individually we are justified and that, individually, we shall go to heaven; and yes, God has a glorious eternal plan for each one of us. But God's vision is much greater. He is restoring the universe. And to care for that, he is bringing into being a new family, a new 'people', a 'new and different society', eager to do good.

The green shape, like the bow of a boat, has now moved to the right of the diagram, as we have seen. This represents the Christian family. I have left it open-ended, because St John tells us that the Christian family is not yet complete and that it will eventually be 'a huge crowd' that no one could count, from every nation in the world.[3] When we are born from above, it's into this family that we are born. Or, to put it differently, if Christ is our Lord and Saviour, whether or not we realise it, we are *already* in the green boat. In the language of the New Testament, we are already in 'the church' – always remembering that the church is a family, never buildings.

Perhaps you are beginning to think, 'Oh dear. Here we go again. He is about to tell me that I *must* go to church.' Not so fast! I welcome the symbol of the bow of a boat because a light-hearted definition of 'fellow-ship' (a New Testament term for Christian sharing) is 'two fellows in a ship'. Why are they both in a ship? Often simply for the fun of it because they both love sailing, and therefore share a 6.05-metre two-man Flying Dutchman. The sharing is therefore the basis of their friendship. It is something like this in the Christian life. You have the Holy Spirit in you. I have the Holy Spirit in me. So we share in the Holy Spirit, and he draws us together in Christian love and in common interests.

I beg you to believe what I am now about to say. Looking back over sixty years of experience of the Christian family, I would say that deep friendship with 'people of the Spirit' has been one of the most enriching parts of my life. And, believe it or not, much of it has been great fun.

Some time ago, I was talking to a fellow Christian. He is an African; I am an Englishman. He is black; I am white. His grandfather had five wives; my grandfather had one. His grandfather was a cannibal; my grandfather enjoyed beef, lamb, and pheasant in season. So we were different. But he loves Jesus; and I love Jesus. He has the Holy Spirit inside him; I have the Holy Spirit inside me. He knows that he's in 'the boat' and so do I. In a few minutes we were talking and laughing together, and I felt closer to him than I do to some of my relations who, alas, are not Christians.

To get a faint notion of what life in the green boat is like, you must picture a small restaurant that has been taken over for the evening by several families who have known and loved each other for many years. The room is packed. There are white heads, grey heads, blonde heads, brunette heads, mousy heads and many little heads. Everybody is talking. Everybody seems to know everybody else and there's a lot of noise. You are surrounded by your own family, who know and love you. The tables are close together and the waiters are rushing round, laughing, cracking jokes and serving up dishes of delicious food to be washed down with red wine. It is a party. And Jesus loved parties. 'I had never previously thought of a laughing, joking Jesus, physically strong and active, fond of good company and a glass of wine, telling funny stories, and holding his companions spellbound with his talk.'[4] So wrote a young man when he first read the Gospel stories in a modern translation. It was during a *supper party*, not in a solemn synagogue service, that Jesus instituted the Holy Communion – a party of close friends to whom he was host. Of course, the terrible events of the following twenty-four hours cast a dark shadow over that particular party.

I am not for a moment suggesting that there is no place for inspiring services in cathedrals and other huge buildings with thousands of worshippers; or for a service of three or four gathered in a village church to meditate quietly as the early morning sunshine streams through the east window. But I *am* saying that Christianity is all about relationships, and that the new life in the Spirit is both a *loving, joyful* relationship with Christ, *and* a *loving, joyful* relationship with his or her family. In addition to formal services, each of us needs a regular *party* of Christians with whom we can make close friends; the sort of party we would never want to miss because of the sheer fun and blessing of it. I add the word 'blessing' because such parties usually include Bible study and an opportunity for the guests to pray for one another. We *need* such a support group. It is worthwhile travelling miles to find it.

Having lived in villages for many years, I would say that being a regular member of the local church is immensely important. How else can we influence our friends and neighbours for Christ? You may think that I am giving the lie to the previous paragraph in which I stressed the importance of joining a small group of Christian friends. Nothing of the kind. With determination and careful planning, we should be able to make room for both.

In cities, circumstances are different. Parochial boundaries have little rhyme or reason. In cities we must look for vibrant spiritual life, and for teaching centred upon Jesus that sends us on our way each Sunday, inspired and encouraged. Occasionally we may even want to visit a church in which most of the congregation are of a different race, colour and social background. This will be exciting, enriching; nearer, too, to the heavenly vision of the church as a 'supranational centre of unity, loyalty and love'.[5] What holds us all together? The golden thread of Jesus.

You may be beginning to think that this is too rosy a picture by half. After all, according to the media, the church is bursting with hypocrites, flat-earthers, and paedophiles. This is not true; but even if it were, one might comment, 'It's the best place for them. There is hope of change!'

For this good reason, in the diagram, all who are 'in Christ' are on the right side of the page, and it is almost impossible to exaggerate the change that has taken place. In St Paul's words, 'If any one is *in Christ*, he is a new creation, the old has passed away, behold, the new has come.'[6] We have crossed the gulf. We are already enjoying '*newness* of life' with the love and support of God's family.

Now we can see why Jesus, when teaching about holy behaviour, pointed to fruit trees. The secret, he said, was to get a good tree: then, in time, there would be plenty of fruit. Once the tree has been 'made good', purely by a miracle of God's grace, fruit would come almost as a by-product – 'of hys owne accorde … without commandment, even of his own nature', as Tyndale put it. We no longer behave like a small child 'for payne of the rod, or for fear of bugges or pleasure of apples'.[7]

St Paul followed this up by giving us a list of the sort of fruit Jesus must have had in mind – not complete, but quite enough to be getting on with. This is such an important aspect of the life of the Spirit that I would encourage you to read through the list slowly, thinking carefully what each word means. Here it is. 'The fruit of the Spirit is love [pause and think], joy [pause and think, and so on], peace, patience, kindness, goodness, faithfulness [or trustworthiness], gentleness and self-control'.[8]

Fruit grows slowly. And this reminds us that there is no short cut to holiness. Growth will continue all our life. Whenever the fruit ripens, *others* enjoy the taste of it.

The first thing I would want to say about this list is that the Apostle is not talking about our feelings – loving *feelings*, joyful *feelings*, peaceful *feelings*, and so on. We are lucky if we have feelings, but, as we all know, feelings come and go. He is talking about action. He is answering such questions as, 'How can I bring joy into my wife's life?' Or, 'How can I show patience to my teenager?' Or, as a driver, 'How may I make the roads safer for others?' On reflection, you might like to go through the list again, even more thoughtfully and imaginatively.

Now here is a possible way of growing more fruit. In the morning, bring to mind the people you are likely to meet during the day. Then ask the Spirit of Jesus (for that is who he is), 'Heavenly Lord, what do you want me to do today to make these people's lives better and to show them your kindness and goodness?' As I do this, I am often surprised by the new thoughts that flow into my mind, and I try to write them down so that I don't forget them before I've done them. They are usually *little* actions, nothing to write home about: 'The trivial round, the common task will furnish all we need to ask,' John Keble sang.[9] And, of course, God may drop into our head such good thoughts at any hour of the day or night.

I must make special mention of 'love', which Paul, like Christ, puts top of his list. What *is* love? A good definition is: 'Love is the accurate estimate and supply of another's need.' Such love will usually require prayer, careful thought, time and trouble.

The head of a firm may have the painful duty of making one of his employees redundant. As a Christian, he knows that it is not enough to tell the man to clear his desk by 5.30 pm. How does he show his Christian love for him? By *feelings* of deep sympathy, whether or not expressed? What good will they do – for the employee, his wife, his children? To make 'an accurate estimate' of his need won't take long. The poor man needs work. Now obviously the employer is not in a position to 'supply the need', but he may be able to help by offering advice and by writing the reference with great care. The point I am trying to make is that the fruit of the Spirit, whether love or one of the others, will always involve self-sacrifice – thought, time, trouble, expense, loss. Look at the list again, and question each 'fruit'. 'How can I bring joy into X's life? How can I reconcile X and Y and make peace between them? I promised I would ring Z this morning. Have I done this – and been trustworthy?'

Now imagine a family, a school, a university college, or an island like the Isle of Wight, where every person was 'in Christ' and every person is hard at work cultivating the fruit of the Spirit: would this not be a dream society, a politician's delight? Wouldn't you want to live there? The police could spend all day filling up forms. Nobody would mind. There would be nothing else for them to do.

There is another way of growing in holiness that I want to touch on. We might call it, 'practising the *Lordship* of Christ'. Jesus once said take 'my yoke, and learn from me, for I am gentle and humble-hearted; and your souls will find rest. For my yoke is good to bear, my load is light.'[10] When a bullock stood still in the farmyard and bent its neck to allow the farmer to put on the yoke, it accepted the farmer's authority. So taking the yoke of Jesus is a powerful picture of obedience.

The poet George Herbert[11] composed a poem called 'The Odour', in which he said that to have Jesus as his master was like walking slowly through an eastern garden, catching the sweet smell of the different flowers. 'How sweetly doth *My Master* sound! *My Master*! ... An oriental fragrancy, *My Master*.'[12] I quote these two lines of the poem to help take the sting out of obedience. The very mention of the word 'obedience', let alone the phrase 'bending the neck', alarms us. Shall we lose out? Will the new master narrow our lives – spoil the fun? George Herbert assures us that not only will he not spoil the fun, but that obeying him will bring a new 'oriental fragrancy' into living. He is 'gentle' and his 'yoke is good to bear', meaning that the yoke fits comfortably and that he will choose the best fields for us to work in.

Nevertheless, I can't entirely take the sting out of obedience. On occasion, it can be a battle. Another poet, George MacDonald,[13] wrote about this in his poem 'Obedience':

I said, 'Let me walk in the fields.'
He said, 'No, walk in the town.'
I said, 'There are no flowers there.'
He said, 'No flowers but a crown.'

I said, 'But the air is thick,
And fog is veiling the sun.'
He answered, 'Yet souls are sick,
And souls in the dark – undone.'

I cast a look at the fields,
Then set my face to the town.
He said, 'My child do you yield?
Will you leave the flowers for the crown?'

Then into his hand went mine;
And into my heart came he;
And I walk in the light divine,
The path I had feared to see.

How and when do we practise the Lordship of Christ? The answer could be, 'when the day breaks'. Before we even open our eyes, while we are still between the sheets, we may greet the Lord by humming a song of praise or the verse of a hymn we might begin with:

Wake, and lift up thyself, my heart,
And with the angels bear thy part
Who all night long, unwearied, sing
High praise to the eternal King.[14]

Both words and tune cheer me and make me smile; and that is good in the early morning. But after a few minutes, we shall want to say, 'My Master, dear Lord, I am glad to be yours, I belong to you – what would *you* like me to do for you today?' Of course I realise that, for most of us, the programme from eight to six (or longer) is largely fixed. But to think that we serve Christ only in the evenings and at the weekend is a mistake of Himalayan proportions. We are serving the Lord in the factory, or in the office, or in playing in an orchestra, *just* as much as when we are in church. And the Christian has a secret, hidden life. As we drive to work, we can keep praising our Master in English, or perhaps more easily (and certainly more safely!) in the language given to us by the Holy Spirit – if we have that gift. Throughout the busy day we can often silently lift our hearts to him for help or guidance. Or we can ask him questions, 'May I do this? May I go there?' and see what he says. Each time we do this, said George Herbert, we will sense a new fragrance in our relationship with Jesus – like passing a honeysuckle bush in full flower.

Of course, the Master will sometimes say 'No'. An Australian had been travelling in Europe. On his way home, he spent a few hours in Switzerland. He was a Christian. He had been working hard. He felt he deserved a treat! In a jeweller's shop window, he noticed a wristwatch. It was chromium plate, with a clear face, a second hand and a dark leather strap – exactly what he wanted. But it was expensive. So he prayed, 'My Master, may I?' The answer was a clear 'No'. He prayed again but, sensing no peace of heart, he turned away and went on to the airport. When he reached home, along with the pile of letters awaiting him, was a small parcel. In it was an affectionate letter from an old friend. And there was more: a watch with a clear face, a second hand and a dark leather strap. This one was 18 carat gold. It had been made by some of the finest craftsmen in Switzerland. Then, how sweetly did 'My Master' sound! 'My Master – an oriental fragrancy.' Let us bring that last phrase up to date. Why the Orient? Why not the fragrancy of an *English* garden – the perfume of a climbing rose and of sweet scented jasmine, intermingled?

By the way, when the Master says, 'No', we don't necessarily get a gold watch! I happen to know that this distinguished Australian lived as simply as possible, often wearing second-hand clothes if he could do so without 'crying poverty', and that he was immensely generous with his money. The Master knew this, too. The yoke of Jesus is 'good to bear'. And that includes treats.

Now put these two pictures of holiness together: the fruit tree and the yoke. Imagine a group of Christians who determine to cultivate the fruit of the Spirit, day after day, month after month. They have also determined to 'bend their necks' and submit to the yoke of Jesus, morning after morning, week after week. What will they be like in six months? Well, you say, they will be *more* like Jesus. And after twenty years? *Even* more like Jesus! I am not trying to weave a spell. This is what actually happens. And can we be *perfectly* like Jesus? No, not until he returns. But then, said St John, 'When [Christ] appears, we shall be like him, for we shall see him as he is.'[15]

I need to say one thing more. It may strike a discordant note, but I will risk it. I have been struck by what scholars call 'the vice lists' in the New Testament. There are a number of them. Some of the sins we would still regard as colourful – what Bunyan describes as sins 'of a bright red colour'. But whether 'off white' or 'bright red', they are always greeted with horror and startled surprise by the New Testament writers. The reaction is, 'How can you as a Christian, knowing what God is like, behave like this? Don't you see how incongruous it is? Don't you see how it must hurt the *Holy* Spirit and dishonour Jesus himself? Stop it! Shun it!'

## *Event 3 continued: Jesus was raised*

### The Christian Family

> *'You are a people holy to the Lord your God. Out of all the peoples on the face of the earth; the Lord has chosen you to be his treasured possession.'*
> Deuteronomy 14:2

> *'So you must live as God's obedient children. Don't slip back into your old ways of living to satisfy your own desires. You didn't know any better then. But now you must be holy in everything you do, just as God who chose you is holy.'*
> 1 Peter 1:14–15, NLT

> *'Aim at a holy life.'*
> Hebrews 12:14, NEB

This takes time and effort.

> *'So, my friends, be obedient ... Work out your salvation in fear and trembling: for it is God who works in you, inspiring both the will and the deed, for his own chosen purpose.'*
> Philippians 2:14, NEB

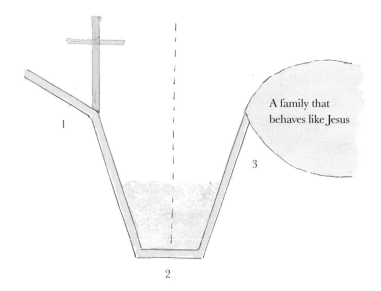

A family that behaves like Jesus

Some of the ways in which Christians become like Christ:

They are ruthless with sin. 'Stop sinning' (John 5:14).

They practise the lordship of Jesus.

They read the Bible and pray.

They cultivate the Fruit of the Spirit.

Here is St Peter's list. He has been writing about building up a loving Christian family. Then he adds, 'rid yourselves of all malice and all deceit, hypocrisy, envy, and slander'.[16] 'If we knew what people said about us behind our back, we would not have a friend in the world,' said Pascal. For good measure, here are three more common failings to be rid of, and which often appear in other lists: quarrelling, stealing, and 'sleeping around' (in the Bible 'fornication', a word that covers all sexual intercourse outside marriage). St Peter says 'Get rid of them', and you will notice that he does not say, 'Stop stealing *gradually*', 'Stop speaking ill of others *gradually*.' He says sharply, 'Stop it. Get rid of it!' He knew well that if we give such habits heart-room, even hidden away on the top floor, they would be bad tenants like moth and mice. They would spoil the home. They might even take over the whole house in time – like dry rot.

St Paul addresses the same problem in his letters. When God transferred us into the kingdom of Jesus, we inevitably took with us patterns of behaviour, memories, tendencies and habits, that we had picked up in the kingdom of darkness. What is a habit? Originally, the word meant what you dress in. It still lingers on with this meaning. She was 'in her riding habit', we say. And, of course, monks still wear a habit. So it's not surprising that St Paul used the same illustration.[17] Before we became Christians, he says, we had a particular wardrobe. And some of these old clothes smell.

A Christian woman who worked in a fish shop used to come to see me in her lunch hour. She brought with her an aroma of stale herring and haddock that quickly permeated the room. Of course, I never mentioned it to her. She couldn't help it, and it was a privilege to talk with her and to have her in our home. However, the children noticed it, and said that my visitor was wearing Chanel Fish No. 5.

But in the Christian life, we *can* help it. Things have come to a pretty pass when Christians smell spiritually offensive, so Paul says, 'Change your clothes. You are new people in Christ. Put off lying, put off anger, put off stealing, put off evil talk (gossip and needless criticism), and put off immorality.'[18] These things stink of the kingdom of darkness. They are like a bundle of dirty old clothes fit only to be rolled up and thrown away. Then, don't sally forth naked! In their place, put on truth, put on forgiveness, put on honest work, put on kindness – and other Christ-like qualities. These are the cool beautiful new clothes of the kingdom of Jesus.

Christians behaving badly are often bewailed by Christian authors. They write, 'Don't these Christians see what they are doing? How can they act so incongruously?' Yet pointing out incongruity does not, alas, help the victim to escape. There is no good news in naming and shaming. But, if we have dared to believe what Christ achieved for us at the cross (Events 1 and

2), if we have learned to battle against the devil (pp. 48–49), if we have discovered the power of the Holy Spirit (which I look forward to writing about in Chapter 6), and if we have made up our mind, with God's help, to have done with ugly things, we shall win.

We really can.[19] We know that this is God's will for us.[20] It will certainly demand determination. It may take a number of hard battles. But this is the way in which we 'cleanse ourselves from *every* defilement of flesh and spirit, perfecting holiness in the fear of God.'[21]

A last word – a word of encouragement. I have known many, many Christians, some of them quite young in the faith. If I had been asked to describe their lives, one word would have jumped to my mind; it is the beautiful New Testament word – blameless. This is how St Paul puts it: 'that you may be *blameless* … children of God … in the midst of a crooked and perverse generation, among whom you shine as lights in the world.'[22]

Like the young Christians whom St John mentions in his first letter, they have overcome the devil. They have fought *and won*.[23]

I said earlier in this chapter that the Christian life was all about relationships, and we are being offered the incomparable privilege of a friendship with God the Father, God the Son, and God the Holy Spirit. Perhaps we ought to have begun there; in the long run, it certainly matters more to us than anything else in the world. How then do we get to know him better?

The answer is that, like all other friendship, we can deepen it only by spending time with him. He speaks to us, and we speak to him.

The chief way in which he speaks to us is through the Bible. Reading the Bible has been likened to reading a daily love letter from Jesus; and this is often so. But sometimes it seems to me more like the careful letter of a parent about marriage; or of a grandparent encouraging us to work hard and to persevere; or of an uncle who knows all about money – its right use and its perils; or even of a friendly police officer who, one day, drops into the kitchen for a cup of tea (as they used to do in country districts) and says, 'If I were you, Miss, I would steer clear of that fellow. 'E's a bad lot, and I wouldn't want to see you in trouble 'cos of 'im.' God adopts all these roles in the Bible, and many more, and when he seems severe, it is only because he loves us and knows that, if we insist on going down a particular road, we are running into serious danger. After all, if a father gives his son a car after passing the test, and then discovers that the boy is repeatedly caught speeding, will he not have something to say to him?

How often should we read the Bible? I have hesitated in answering this question ever since I met a young officer in the merchant navy. You will see why in a moment. Malcolm was an outstanding man with a fine career ahead of him. Then things went wrong. He began to drink heavily and ended up seriously ill.

In hospital he fell in love with beautiful Jane, the night nurse, and asked her to marry him. Jane was a Christian, so she said, 'I like you very much, but when you are well enough you will have to meet my family and come to church with me, and then we'll see.' Six weeks later, he came out of hospital. It was a Sunday, and at the church there was a visiting preacher named John Stott. Many years later, Jane wrote to me and told me what happened. The story goes like this:

Dear John,

Malcolm wanted me to meet his parents who lived in Yorkshire. I wanted to hear John Stott. I said I would go up north with him on the condition he came to church with me. Yes, he was reluctant, as he had given up one girlfriend because she was a Christian and here he was caught by another. God pursues us, I know; he did me as well. He was amazed by the sermon and we sat in the train all the way up to Hull, which in those days took forever, talking Jesus. I bought him the Bible before he went back to sea and still have it somewhere with all the notes in.

Many blessings and lots of love, Jane

Now if I had known, that Sunday evening, that Malcolm had prayed that he might be a follower of

Jesus all his life, and *if* I had been asked to give him the benefit of my advice, I would probably have said to him, 'Malcolm, here is a New Testament. Start reading, and I suggest you try to read it for ten minutes each day.' Fortunately, I never met him that evening. When Malcolm returned to his ship, Jane gave him a Bible, and simply said, 'Read it.' So, not having the benefit of my advice, when he arrived on board he said to himself, 'I wonder how long I should read each day?' He decided that two hours a day when he was off duty would be about right!

Three months later, he came to see me and told me his story. I was astonished at his Christian maturity. He had been reading, or rather soaking himself in, God's written word – and obeying it. So his life was rapidly being changed and transformed into what God wanted him to be. Shortly afterwards, Malcolm and Jane were married.

So what I am saying is read the Bible as much as you can. You may not, like Malcolm, have the time to read it for hours. But you can *choose* to read *every day* – preferably alone – or if not alone, on the bus (you will need a pocket New Testament), on the train, on the underground, over lunch, from a CD when you are driving, from a Bible study on the internet, or from a verse stuck on the mirror as you are dressing in the morning. Even this last could be a spiritual snack, like a glass of fresh orange juice instead of a full breakfast. Also, you can *determine* to learn important verses by heart.

Write them in a notebook and revise them regularly until you know them for life. You can then chew over them as you go about; they will strengthen you, like the best rump steak. You will have realised that the Bible is a library of books. So, although one day you will find a bird's eye view of the Bible invaluable, don't begin by trying to read it from Genesis to Revelation: you are almost bound to get stuck. The intelligent way to use a library is to read one book at a time. Somebody has pointed out that 'the Bible is a book with the answers at the back,' which is a way of saying that we shall make life easier for ourselves if we begin with the New Testament. So why not embark on one of the Gospels or on the short letter 1 Peter? Be sure to equip yourself with a modern translation, and it may help you to have some explanatory notes.

So God speaks to us, chiefly through the Bible. He also loves to speak to us by the Spirit, and I will have something to say about listening to the Spirit when we reach Event 5.

But to make it a real relationship, *we* obviously have to speak to *him*. Initially there is a strangeness about talking to somebody we cannot see. Nevertheless, if we grasped the astonishing teaching of Event 1 (justification by grace and faith) we will, without realising it, already have stumbled upon the best foundation for Christian prayer.

Abraham discovered this secret. He did so because there was a deep sadness in his life. He longed for his wife, Sarah, to have a baby boy. They had been trying for many years without success. Then, on one of those clear nights when the stars seem very near, he was standing outside his tent in the desert. And God spoke to him – by name for the first time. 'You see the stars, Abraham. Have a good look at them.' (Even without a telescope he would have been able to see seven thousand or so – enough to be going on with.) 'You are going to have as many descendants as the stars in the sky.'

Please notice that Abraham did nothing. We often think that God is pleased with what we do. Well, he may be. But Abraham's reaction was different. He didn't rush about. He simply stood at the door of his tent, and said, 'Lord, I believe you. I trust you utterly.'

It was not only trusting the promise, though it *was* that. 'He believed *the Lord*.' He passed through the promise and embraced God as his Father. And we are told in the story that God accepted this childlike trust as 'righteousness'; the same righteousness, (sharply distinguished from our own feeble efforts to be good) – exactly the same astonishing 'justification by grace and faith' that Jesus and St Paul taught 1,900 years or so later.

Now do you remember that when we were studying justification by grace and faith in Chapter 1, I pointed out that this was the one perfect relationship in the world, and that it would not be more perfect in heaven? So begin to pray with that thought; 'Lord, I am in a perfect relationship with you.' And *begin to pray today*, asking the Holy Spirit to help you.

You might start, 'Father', or 'Lord Jesus', if you prefer, 'I can't see you, but I *know* that I'm in your presence, that you accept me, that you are listening and that you love me … .' Abraham must have begun in some such way, and notice that each of those last four sentences (beginning with 'I'm in your presence …') is an expression of faith. We are told in the New Testament that faith 'pleases' God. So God must have been very pleased. He must have said to himself, 'Here, at last, is a man who listens to me (even when I tell him something very difficult to believe), trusts me and therefore obeys me, and talks to me naturally.' And Abraham kept it up. He talked to God, and he went on talking to God – sometimes shortly, sometimes at length; sometimes about the things that he knew interested God, sometimes about the things that interested himself; sometimes even boldly arguing with God, like a present-day Riyadh carpet dealer: polite, with a twinkle in his eye, but determined to win if he could; in other words, real conversation between a real God and a real man. And there are little hints in the narrative that God loved these conversations. That is what prayer is. Needless to say, as the years went by, Abraham grew to know God better and better. Is it surprising, therefore, that he is the only man in the Bible who three times is called 'God's friend'? This was done twice by men and once by God himself: 'Abraham, my friend.' What a privilege!

I cannot think of a nobler ambition in life than this. That when we eventually meet God face to face, He will say to us, 'George, my friend. Elizabeth, my friend.'

This has become a long chapter. I can't help it. Christianity is not a little matter; it is titanic – embracing what we do every moment of the day. But I wonder whether you are beginning to see that, in this new life on the right side of the diagram, the Holy Spirit is inviting us, like skilled surfers, to ride on huge waves of love, sacrifice and power of which the world, before Christ came, scarcely dreamed?

## *Believing pages*

*'He has rescued us from the dominion of darkness
and brought us into the kingdom of the Son he
loves ... .'*
Colossians 1:13

Do you believe this? Do you believe that, in
the diagram you have crossed the gulf, and
that you are 'in Christ' and on the right side
of the page?

The devil will do his best to persuade
you that you are still on the left side; that
you are 'the same as you always were';
that there is no change and that you are
under his power; or that you are sometimes
in one kingdom and sometimes in the other.
These are all lies. So, even when we fail, and
the devil accuses us, we must stand our ground.
The truth is that we are in the kingdom of
Jesus. That is how we must always think of
ourselves; because that is where we are.

A prayer to pray, very slowly, line by line:

*Heavenly Father,
In Jesus, you carried me across the gulf.
I believe that I am now in your eternal kingdom.*

*I believe that I am one of your people, and that heaven is my home.*
*I believe that I am a sheep in your flock, that you know me by name.*
*I believe that I am a branch in the vine that will produce much fruit.*
*I believe that I am cared for, valued, watched over, loved.*
*Heavenly Father, I am so grateful. Thank you.*
*Amen.*

## Three further prayers

*Father, guide me to members of your family who mirror the joy of heaven, and who display the love that flows between you, the Lord Jesus, and the Holy Spirit. Amen.*

*Lord Jesus, whether you call me to be a politician or a policewoman, a dustman or a doctor, a teacher or a tailor, a secretary or a soldier, may I glorify you by what I do, and please you by the way I do it. Amen.*

*Holy Spirit, you who helped Jesus to fight the devil in the wilderness, and to win, please search my heart, and give me the power and the courage to break any bad habit, and to destroy any stronghold that the enemy clings to in my life. Amen.*

# *Notes*

1. John 3:3 ff.
2. Tim Raikes, published in *The Spectator*, 21 August 2010.
3. Revelation 7:9.
4. Lord Hailsham, *The Door Wherein I Went* (Fountain Paperbacks, 1978), p.57.
5. Lesslie Newbigin, in a statement on international peace at the SCM conference in 1934.
6. 2 Corinthians 5:17 (RSV, my italics).
7. Not bugs; but probably from the Old English word 'boogges' – meaning a terrifying spectre. Cp. 'Thou shalt not nede to be afrayed for any bugges by night.' Tyndale's translation of Psalm 91:15.
8. Galatians 5:22–23.
9. Poet, hymn writer and scholar (1792–1866).
10. Matthew 11:29, NEB, but 'rest' has been used rather than 'relief'.
11. 1593–1632.
12. George Herbert, *The Works*, Vol. II (William Pickering, 1846), p.200.
13. 1824–1905.
14. Awake my soul …', Bishop Thomas Ken (1637–1711) of Bath and Wells (1684–1689). In 1683 he refused the use of his house to the royal mistress, Nell Gwyn. Tune: Morning Hymn.
15. 1 John 3:2.
16. 1 Peter 2:1.
17. Eg Ephesians 4:22ff. NB Put off. (22) Put on. (24) Putting away … (25), Put away. (31) And put on the opposite characteristics.
18. See 1 Corinthians 6:10–11 and 2 Corinthians 12:20–21.
19. Some problems are very severe. We may need the advice, and the prayers and help of mature and experienced Christians. The sooner we get this the better.
20. 1 Thessalonians 4:3: 'For this is the will of God, your sanctification' (NRSV). See also 1 Thessalonians 3:13.
21. 2 Corinthians 7:1; 'Flesh' translates the word *sarx*.
22. Philippians 2:15 (RSV, my italics).
23. 1 John 2:13 and 14.

*Chapter 4*

# Jesus Ascended

Some months ago, three businessmen met me at 8:15 in the evening. We opened a bottle of wine, ate chocolate pudding together, read a passage from St John's Gospel, and discussed it in some depth. When we had finished, one of the men said wistfully, 'It would be easy to stay in God's presence if I read the Bible all day, or sat in a church all day. But life's not like that. The people I work with are a godless lot. To be honest,' he added, 'I usually forget God from Monday morning to Saturday night. I can't help it.'

So do saintly Christians think consciously of God *all* day? Not being one of them, I don't know. They may do; at least they may do so more than others. But, in a business committee, even a saintly Christian will have to concentrate on the matter in hand or he will lose money; equally in an exam or she will lose marks. It is, I think, more like being in Switzerland. You don't look at the mountains all the time. But you are always aware that the snow-capped peaks are above you. You know that they are there – even at night. So it was an important question for my business friend to ask, 'Is it possible to have that sort of *awareness* of God in an office with difficult colleagues, or on the factory floor, or fighting in the army, or while caring for three small, fractious children?'

The early Christians knew the answer to this question. It is linked with the ascension of Jesus – represented by the upward leap of the diagram between points 3 and 4 (see p. 105). At the ascension, you may remember, a cloud came over the hill and hid Jesus 'as he was taken up'. But what became of Jesus? What happened next contains the answer to the businessman's question. Nobody could have guessed it. Indeed, if God had not told the apostles, we would never have known this fascinating secret.

Perhaps the best way to grasp what I am talking about is for me to ask another question – a much duller one: 'Where are you sitting?' 'Well,' you reply, 'I am sitting at my desk. Or I am sitting in an easy chair. Or I am not sitting at all; I'm standing in a crowded train.'

We will return to my dull question later on, but here I must draw attention to two beautiful words in the New Testament. They are, 'But God … .' St Paul had been describing how God viewed sinful humanity, and despite humanity's brilliance, and astonishing achievements, it's a devastating assessment. 'You were dead', he writes – *spiritually* dead.

In the first parish I served, the dead were usually kept in the house until burial. So when I called to offer what comfort I could, to talk about the funeral and to pray for the family, the widow often said to me, 'Would you like to see the body, Sir?' Not wanting to hurt her, I always said, 'Yes'. We then went into the little front room. It was dominated by the coffin. She would remove the lid. And there was the corpse: eyes closed, yellow skin, sunken cheeks, the bones of the nose more prominent, an unpleasant smell not entirely masked by the undertaker's skill. Dead. I felt so sorry for the poor widow and often, quite spontaneously, put my arm round her and gave her a gentle hug. But I was glad to get out of the room, into the fresh air, away from the presence of death. And that, said the apostle, is how God viewed us – spiritually; 'dead ... dead in our sins'. A corpse doesn't pray. A corpse doesn't hear God. A corpse can't see the kingdom. So to a spiritual corpse (however lively, intelligent, and gifted a particular corpse may *appear* to be), is it surprising that Christianity usually seems 'boring, untrue and irrelevant'?[1]

And now, in startling juxtaposition to the phrase 'dead in sins', come the two beautiful words, 'But God ... .' 'But God, in his great love for us,' the passage continues. (So, he loves us; he loves *you*. You believe that, don't you? 'Yes,' you say!) Consequently, 'in his great love', he *did* something. He *acted*. He not only raised the dead Jesus from the grave and 'made *him* sit in heavenly places', he did the same for *us*. The moment we put our trust in Christ and surrender to him, God swoops down, opens our spiritual coffins, and, as we have joyously experienced, brings us to life, see Event 3 in the diagram. 'But God ...' doesn't even stop there. He goes further. In his great love, 'God raised us up with Christ and seated us with him in the heavenly realms in Christ.'[2] God exalts us, God dignifies us; and heavenwards we go – soaring up – to sit next to Jesus himself.

## Event 4: Jesus ascended

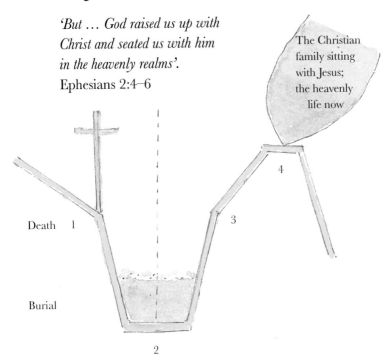

'But ... God raised us up with Christ and seated us with him in the heavenly realms'.
Ephesians 2:4–6

The Christian family sitting with Jesus; the heavenly life now

Death    1

3

4

Burial

2

This is not the privilege of a few model Christians. God has raised us *all* in Christ. We are already citizens of heaven. Heaven is now our true home. We are foreigners in this world, pilgrims passing through it. Sometimes we feel this acutely. Like Abraham we are looking for 'a better country' (Hebrews 11:16), 'a city not made with hands'. Those who have seen this truth most clearly, have usually been amongst those who have served their own age most heroically (Philippians 3:20–21; Hebrews 11:8, 10, 13).

This, I assure you, is not some quaint mystical idea. It has profound practical consequences for daily living. Nor is it something that will happen at death, or that God will do in the distant future. He *has* done it already. Where St Paul describes God's action in his letter to the Ephesians, the three verbs 'he brought to life', 'he raised', 'he seated' are all in the aorist tense. That is to say, the action took place in the past, in a moment of time.

So how does God regard us now? Spiritually alive; and, more than that, we are sitting high up, in a place of honour very close to Jesus. To this movement from the left side of the diagram to the right side, and then upward, we have contributed absolutely nothing – except our sins. It is totally and utterly *God's* loving goodness. *He* has put us there.

Early in his Christian life, Billy Bray came to realise this. Billy was born at Twelveheads, a village near Truro in Cornwall on the 1 June 1794. Politicians today are interested in 'class'; some like to claim that they are 'middle class', or (even better) 'lower middle class'. Billy was the lowest of the low. He was 'a tinner', or miner, working underground in the tin mines. He was also a womaniser and a drunkard. Night after night, his wife had to fetch him home from the beer shop. Of the bad men in the area, he was the wildest. But, drunk or sober, he was full of fun and splendid company.

In the summer of 1823, a little book by John Bunyan entitled *Visions of Heaven and Hell* fell into his hands. Billy read it, and on the next payday, for the first time for many years, he came home sober. His wife said to him, 'How is it that you are home so early tonight?' He replied, 'By the help of the Lord, you will never see me drunk again.'

Day after day he knelt by his bedside reading the Bible, reading his hymnbook, and crying to God for mercy; and then, sometime in November 1823, it happened. In his own words:

I said to the Lord, 'Thou hast said, they that
ask shall receive, they that seek shall find, and
to them that knock the door shall be opened',[3]
and I have faith to believe it. In an instant the
Lord made me so happy that I cannot express
what I felt. I shouted for joy. I praised God with

> my whole heart for what he had done for a
> poor sinner like me. I could say, 'The Lord hath
> pardoned all my sins.'[4]

Now if you had met Billy Bray at Christmas 1823 and asked him what 'class' he came from, he would have said (with a twinkle in his eye) 'I am a young Prince'.

Filled with the Holy Spirit, he knew that he was a son of the King of kings, that heaven was his true home, and that God had 'made him' – a tinner – sit next to Christ. This gave him the confidence to go anywhere and speak about Jesus to anybody. He was not ashamed to go to big houses in Cornwall to ask for money for poor families and other good causes. A friend once suggested that he should go to the back door. 'No,' said Billy, 'I am a King's son, and I shall go frontways.' He suffered much ridicule and opposition. Yet when he died in 1868, he, the humblest of men, was known and loved throughout Cornwall. The title of his biography is *The King's Son*.

This is the way – and I can't emphasise this too strongly – this is the way in which we, too, should always think of ourselves. And notice the immediate consequence. It is so obvious that I need scarcely state it. We become aware that Jesus is very near us. God has 'seated us' or 'enthroned us' *with him*. We are the sons and daughters of the King of kings. He can whisper to us at any time. Equally, we can whisper to him. And even when these secret conversations are not going on, we know that he is there.

Now you remember the problem raised by the businessman at the beginning of this chapter: Is it possible to enjoy the presence of God all day in a secular world – working on the factory floor, fighting in the army and so on? What do you think?

The moment has come for me to return to what I called my 'dull' question. I will ask it again. Where are you sitting? And if you reply, '*I think* I see what you are saying, but how do I get there?' I shall be strongly tempted to let fly at you (lovingly, of course!) as did Bishop Latimer with his sixteenth-century country congregations, 'Ye hoddy-pecks, ye huddes, ye doddy-pouls, do ye not understand?'[5]

Because, in Christ, *we are there*. God has done it. God has made us sit with Christ. It is his grace, his love and his kindness. All we have to do is to dare to believe *what God has done*. And live it out, as Brother Lawrence did. What particularly inspires and encourages me is this. You remember his well known words: that his awareness of the presence of God was such that 'he was unable to say whether it had increased or decreased over a period of forty years;' and that he possessed this awareness 'in as great tranquillity in the noise and clutter of the kitchen as when he was on his knees in chapel.'[6] This awareness of God's presence is usually held up as something exceptional, an experience that only Christians who have achieved 99 per cent in sanctification might enjoy. In fact, the apostles seem to have taught it as standard run-of-the-mill Christianity.

In the third-century liturgy of St Hipollytus, the words rang out, 'Lift up your hearts,' and the people replied, 'We have them in the presence of the Lord.' I think – don't you? – that they knew where they were sitting.

## *Believing pages*

*'But because of his great love for us … .'*
Ephesians 2:4

Do you believe this? Do you believe that God loves you?

A teenage boy in the youth club said to his vicar, 'You know, Vicar, God likes you. He really does. He likes you very much indeed.' Now the vicar had believed for many years that God loved him. But this remark struck a new note in his thinking. It warmed his heart. Never before had he thought that God liked him.

Do you believe that God likes you?

*'God raised us up with Christ and seated us with him in the heavenly realms in Christ Jesus.'*
Ephesians 2:6

Do you believe this for yourself? So where are you sitting?

A businessman kept on his desk a small card, attractively framed. On it were printed the words, 'Keep looking down!' Some of his colleagues understood: but not all.

In Jesus, we are also 'far above' the powers of darkness (cp Ephesians 1:19ff). However much we are attacked, we can push them down. West Indians dramatise this by stamping with their feet as they sing their songs of victory. The powers of darkness are like ill-bred dogs that scrabble on us with dirty paws. Speak to them with confidence and authority, 'Down! Down! In Jesus' Name.'

A prayer to pray – slowly, savouring each line:

> *Heavenly Father, we are amazed at your love.*
> *Thank you for calling us your people.*
> *Thank you for knowing each one of us by name.*
> *And Lord, I can scarcely believe it –*
> *But thank you for loving me; thank you for liking me.*
> *I believe that you have honoured me by raising me to sit with Jesus.*
> *Close to him, on his throne: the place of rest, of prayer, of power.*
> *Help me always to believe this, always to think like this,*
> *Always to live like this. In Jesus' Name and for his glory, Amen.*

# *Notes*

1. Nicky Gumbel, *Questions of Life* (Alpha International, 2010), chapter 1.

2. Ephesians 2:6.

3. Luke 11:9, 13. A passage in which Jesus says how willing God is to give the Holy Spirit to those who ask him.

4. *Billy Bray: The King's Son* (F. W. Bourne, Simpkin, Marshall, Hamilton and Kent, 1896), p.10.

5. What do these words mean? I have no idea. Your guess is as good as mine.

6. Brother Lawrence, *The Practice of the Presence of God* (Hodder and Stoughton, 2009), page number unknown.

*Chapter 5*

# Jesus Poured Out the Holy Spirit

We have reached the fifth and final leg of the diagram. It now turns *downward* because, as soon as Jesus had returned to his Father, he poured out the Holy Spirit upon the world. After Jesus went *up*, the Holy Spirit came *down*. God's sublime purpose is that the Christian family, a family of every race and colour, should be filled with the third glorious Person of the Trinity. That includes you and me. In fact, the previous four Events of the diagram – the death, burial, resurrection and ascension of Jesus – took place, to some degree, *in order* that we might be filled with the Spirit of Jesus. Jesus came 'the fire celestial to impart',[1] a thrilling moment for the world.

Now I have to confess to you that, at some points, my diagram breaks down. As you look back over the five legs, you might be forgiven for thinking that the Holy Spirit has had nothing to do with you until this fifth leg.

That would be ludicrously wrong. God has sometimes been compared to a master chess player, moving us about on the board of life so that eventually we come face to face with Jesus; this being the secret work of the Holy Spirit. This is absolutely true; but unfortunately, it suggests that we are helpless pawns in God's hand. Not so. He has given us a measure of free will, and he always honours our choices. Exactly how these two – God's sovereignty and our free will – come together in daily life is a mystery.[2] Occasionally we catch a glimpse of the Spirit's presence, like the glint of a submarine's periscope as it disappears beneath the waves. (Was it a periscope, or did we imagine it?). We experience an odd coincidence, protection in a moment of danger, or we hear a sermon that seemed to be addressed, personally, to me. (Who briefed the speaker?) All this is the work of the Spirit. Or we discover that a parent, or a great aunt, or a friend has been praying for us for many years, and we suspect that it was these prayers that have enabled the Holy Spirit to work so powerfully in our life. We change our mind about Christianity. This too is the work of the Spirit. We pray, 'Lord Jesus, be *my* Lord, be *my* Saviour.' That, above all, is the work of the Spirit. And yet, even then, we may scarcely be aware of his presence. We often sing at Christmas, 'How silently, how silently, the wondrous gift is given; so God imparts to human hearts the blessings of his heaven.'[3] This, generally, is true.

## *Event 5: Jesus poured out the Holy Spirit*

Jesus poured out his Holy Spirit, and we can be filled with the Holy Spirit.

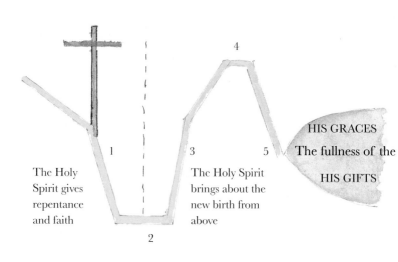

The Holy Spirit opens our eyes to points 1, 2, 3 and 4.

For others, meeting with Jesus, being born from above, and being filled with the Spirit, come together in a memorable spiritual experience. God has intervened in their lives, and they know it.[4] In the New Testament such people often receive a spiritual enhancer, as we might say today – a healing, a vision, or a new language given by the Holy Spirit. I was in Jerusalem when, for the first time, and to my great surprise, I encountered this last gift.

A cultured American woman, the wife of a senior officer in the USA Navy, was deeply concerned about another member of the party. We both knew something of the problem and she asked me whether we might pray about it together. I agreed and we went to a private room in the hotel. First, I prayed. Then she prayed, in English, of course. When I thought she was about to say 'through Jesus Christ, our Lord, Amen', she paused for a moment and then continued in another language. It was beautiful and musical. I wondered if it was modern Greek. I assumed that she was bilingual and made no comment. Two days later, she was sitting next to me in a bus. By way of conversation, I said, 'Do tell me. What is your other language?' 'Oh', she replied, blushing slightly, 'I didn't really mean you to hear that. You are a vicar and some vicars don't approve! It's a language of praise given to me fifteen years ago, when I was filled with the Holy Spirit. You can't praise God too much, you know.'[5] I was fascinated.

That was nearly fifty years ago. Today, countless Christians from all around the world, including many bishops and Christian leaders, have received this gift – the same gift that was given when the Holy Spirit was first poured out in Acts, chapter 2.

Sometimes a different gift is given. There was a man named Keith. He worked in a team of tough men in a large garage. He often used to come to see me. He told me that he never seemed able to influence the other men for Christ. However, he refused to be discouraged, and there came a day when Keith was filled with the Spirit. Shortly after, at the end of a hard day's work, he went home in the evening and sat down in his room to rest. Suddenly, (and I assure you Keith was no dreamer, no visionary) in his own words, 'the heavens were opened, and he heard the angels singing'. He came hurrying up to the vicarage on his bicycle. I was out, but he told my wife his extraordinary experience, how he had glimpsed the heavenly world. Then he added, 'Mrs Collins, does this *often* happen to the vicar?' She had to confess, that, as far as she knew, it had never happened to the vicar. Nor had it! Keith's faith rose. He knew that God was with him. He helped two men to become Christians in the following year. I hope that you enjoy these stories as much as I do. They strengthen my faith, and remind me that anything that happened in the New Testament could happen today. Let me tell you one more.

There was a man whose home was surrounded by tall trees. He asked a group of men to visit him and to pray for him that he might be filled with the Spirit. They did so, and laid their hands on his head. He wrote afterwards, 'Almost immediately, all awareness of the men, of their prayers, of the room, even of myself, was overshadowed by the immense sense of the presence of God. The very foundation of my soul shook violently. A few minutes later, I thought to myself, "If I had wings to carry me to the top of the nearest tree, I would proclaim the praises of God for miles around." '

In these stories, three people experienced God in different ways. The first was given a new language that became part of her devotional life. The second caught a glimpse of the heavenly world, and was empowered for evangelism. The third was overwhelmed with praise. So our experiences vary. Indeed, there seems to be a tailor-made experience for each of us. We are different temperamentally, and what suits you may not suit me, and what suits me may not suit you. Sometimes the Holy Spirit comes as a dove (bringing peace), sometimes as fire (to burn up any rubbish), sometimes as oil (to heal), sometimes as water (to refresh), sometimes as wind (to empower) and sometimes as love poured out.

I would also want to say that, normally in the Christian life, 'we walk by faith'. What is walking? A step in the right direction. What is faith? Trusting God, and trusting what he says, whatever we feel. So faith and obedience are very close. Faith may *seem* like a leap in the dark; but it is always a leap made in obedience to the voice of God. His voice shines through the darkness from his written word, the Bible.

Nevertheless, having said this, I have to insist that we are not filled with the glorious third Person of the Trinity *imperceptibly.* There is a largeness, a lavishness, a generosity in the terms used – The Holy Spirit *'falls'.*

He is '*poured out*'. These last two words are used by Paul. He writes about the 'love of God *poured* into our hearts by the Holy Spirit'. This is not something to argue about. We have either experienced it, or we have not.

All Christians believe in the fullness of the Holy Spirit. Some think that it is a matter of our capacity, and that it is possible to receive him so minimally that there is little difference. Well, there may be a grain of truth in this and I will say something about it later; but this is not spiritual health as God intended. In the New Testament, people seemed to know when they were filled with the Spirit. It is the same today. We will know when 'we are clothed with power from on high' and so will others; indeed, others are likely to be the first to notice it. Jesus didn't say to his disciples, 'Wait until you *think* that you *may possibly* be clothed with power from on high.' A wife will know when her husband is filled with the Spirit. A husband will know when his wife is filled with the Spirit. Even your dog and cat will notice. You may think that I am joking but I am not. Animals are sensitive to good and evil. A diocesan exorcist once told me that his tomcat would be as friendly as a hornet's nest when a demonised person came into the office. It would shrink into a corner, hair on end, spitting and swearing, its tail like a fox's brush. So is it surprising that, when the Spirit of Jesus is powerfully present, animals love it? Or rather, that they love him in us?

Now, some of you are reading this book because you have been filled with the Spirit. God met you when you were praying alone, or at the time of your confirmation, or in a church service, or when taking part in Alpha, or while walking along a busy city street. You realised that something wonderful had happened. Since then you have been learning to walk by faith.

Others may not be sure. So I want now to direct your attention to one of the most remarkable things that Jesus ever said: 'If any one thirst, let him come to me and drink. He who believes in me, as the scripture has said, "Out of his heart shall flow rivers of living water."' St John adds a comment: 'this he [Jesus] said about the Spirit, which those who believed in him were to receive; for as yet the Spirit had not been given, because Jesus was not yet glorified.'[6] (That is, Jesus had not yet been crucified, been raised from the dead or ascended into heaven.)

These are golden words; a stupendous invitation. Let me expand it a little for you. 'If *any* man, *any* woman ... .' We don't have to be special. 'Any' will do.

There is one qualification. Thirst. 'If any one *thirst* ... .' We speak of *burning* thirst. To be without water in a desert or on a raft at sea under a blazing sun is torment. We would do anything for a glass of fresh water. So when Jesus uses 'thirst' with several delicate shades of meaning, there is always a pain, always an urgency about each one. Thirst for God (I long to know God, and to be sure that he has forgiven and accepted me. Events 1 and 2). Thirst for satisfaction (I long for Jesus to take away my frustrations and unsatisfied hungers, and to give me the sort of life that deep down I have always wanted to live. Events 3 and 4). I realise that this sounds selfish, but I am also aware that, if the prodigal son had waited for lofty motives, he would still be in the pigsty. Or thirst for usefulness (I long to be useful, and, as I scrutinise my life, to know that it has some significance, however small, before it peters away into dotage. Event 5).

Well, you can be absolutely sure that God wants all these things for us. In particular, he wants to use us. Or, if I may be even more personal, he wants to use *you*.

This last desire is closely linked with the Lordship of Jesus. Inevitably: because God will never rob us of free will. It is all too easy for us to murmur, 'Jesus, be my Lord,' without realising what a very big prayer this is to pray. Yet without *understanding* and *meaning* what we are saying, our usefulness to God is bound to be severely hampered. So how should we pray? To spell it out: 'Jesus, be my Lord' will cover such prayers as these. Be Lord of my thinking. Be Lord of my career. Be Lord of my friendships. Be Lord of my sex life. Be Lord of my marriage. Be Lord of my home. Be Lord of my work. Be Lord of my ambitions. Be Lord of my money. Be Lord of my spare time. Be Lord of my holidays; and so on. Some of those petitions are hard – a sort of death. We shall be dreadfully tempted to say, 'One day perhaps, Lord, but please not yet.' Some prayers will need to be repeated, and new prayers added as our circumstances change and our understanding increases. These are prayers to pray very slowly. The rub is to add the word '*all*'. 'Lord Jesus, be Lord of *all*.' And yet ... and yet ... how can we give less? 'Love so amazing, so divine, demands my life, my soul, my *all*.'[7] Does it not?

I have wondered if the words 'hard' and 'a sort of death' are too strong? I don't think so. Nicky Gumbel puts his finger on why we quake and shrink back from one or other of these petitions. 'The trouble,' he writes, 'is that we feel that we can improve on God's plan for our lives. We think, "I can do a little better than God; that God is a bit out of touch. He hasn't caught up with the modern world and the things that we enjoy. At least in some areas, I will run my own life, and keep God well out."' To this battle of faith (for that is what it is) I would gladly give a little ease if I can. I would say, 'Oh, don't turn back. That way is loss. Pray earnestly that God will make you willing.' For, as he adds, 'God only wants us to entrust our lives to him so that we can discover how *perfect* his plan is.'[8] Richard Foster goes even further. He simply says, 'Abandon yourself to God. And do it with celebration. Make it a merry revolt against pride and selfishness.' Surely he's right. Laugh and do it![9]

I now go back to the golden words of Jesus, 'If anyone thirst, let him come unto me.' They have a background. When Jerusalem was destroyed by the Babylonians in 587 BC, Ezekiel, one of the great Old Testament prophets, had a vision. He saw a new Temple. It stood at the top of a high mountain, and was even more beautiful than Solomon's. As Ezekiel watched, he saw a trickle of water emerging from under the Temple gate. Every moment the water deepened, first ankle deep, then knee deep, then waist deep, until it became a river in which you could swim. And as the river swept down through the thirsty wilderness to the Dead Sea, Judea became, once again, like the garden of Eden. This vision was six hundred years old. Many Jews remembered it. They thought that when the Messiah came, it would be fulfilled – literally.

Do you begin to see how this invitation of Jesus picks up this unlikely vision of water pouring out from a Temple on a mountain top and transfigures it? It becomes a promise of hope and joy for *any* man or *any* woman in the world.

For what was God's address in the Old Testament? 'If I had wanted to meet God in those far off days,' you reply, 'I would have gone to the Temple.' And if the date had been AD 28, what then? 'I would have gone to Jesus: because God lived in him.' That is absolutely right. So what about today? Where does God live today? And the answer, as you know, is so astonishing that I want to jump up and shout aloud with joy and gratitude. It is nothing less than that God lives in a man, *any* man, or in a woman, *any* woman, cleansed by the cross of Jesus and indwelt by the Spirit. Or, better still, God lives in a *great company* of men and women, the body of Christ, cleansed by the cross of Jesus and filled with the Spirit.

So when Jesus went on to say, 'Out of his heart will flow rivers of living water', he was foreseeing that when *any* man drank of the water of Spirit, that water would first become a fountain *in* him (cleansing, satisfying) and then (providing him with a noble, lifelong task) overflowing *out* of him in every direction, like rivers, bringing health, not to rocky hills and a strip of desert near the Dead Sea, but to the wastelands of spiritually thirsty men and women the world over.

More than that, we catch a new glimpse of the church – a Temple on a mountaintop, splendid, awe-inspiring. Its influence sweeps 'down the centuries' (like a great river down the mountain side) as the church leaps forward with 'anthems and shining crosses and steady-eyed saints. No longer [is] the faith something for children: intelligent people [hold] it strongly – they walk to a secret singing that [the world cannot] hear' and wherever the river flows, trees spring up bearing fruit for the healing of the nations.[10]

Malcolm Muggeridge was born into a strongly political home. In his autobiography he says that he was brought up to believe that Jesus was 'a most high-minded man … who might well have ended up as the Honourable Member for Galilee South'.

After Cambridge, MI5 during the war, a brilliant career as journalist and becoming editor of *Punch*, he eventually became a Christian. As he looked back over his life, this is what he wrote:

> I may, I suppose, regard myself, or pass for being, a relatively successful man. People occasionally stare at me in the street – that's fame. I can fairly easily earn enough to qualify for admission to the higher slopes of the Inland Revenue – that's success … . It might happen once in a while that something I wrote or said was sufficiently heeded for me to persuade myself that it represented a serious impact on our time – that's fulfilment. Yet I say to you – and I beg you to believe me – multiply these tiny triumphs by a million, add them all together, and they are nothing, less than nothing, a positive impediment, measured against one draught of that *Living Water* Christ offers to the spiritually thirsty, irrespective of who or what they are.[11]

Or look at it another way. If God the Holy Spirit pays us the almost intolerable compliment of *filling us with himself*, he does it primarily not to give us an exciting experience, or that we may swing on the chandeliers, though he may allow us to do so for a week or two because we are so overwhelmed with the joy of the Lord. He does it in order to get his work done in the world.

It is like falling in love. Without that magical spark, few would have the courage to embark on lifelong marriage. But when love comes, they launch out. They can't wait.

And there is so much to be done. We all know friends and neighbours who are destroying their lives, their marriages, and the lives of their children because they have drifted and drifted until any Christianity they ever knew seems a distant, irrelevant memory. I need say no more. Why should we unnerve one another with gloomy statistics of murders, rapes, and child abuse? We can leave that to the television. What the Holy Spirit of Jesus did in the Acts of the Apostles, followed by the story of how he transformed the Roman empire in less than three hundred years, tells us that these dismal problems can be overcome. The Light can still shine. The darkness can still be chased away *if, and only if,* Christian people (whatever else they do or don't do) 'hunger and thirst' until in St Luke's words 'they are clothed with power from on high'.

So we must return to the question, 'How can I be filled with the Holy Spirit?'

The answer, as so often in the Christian life, is profoundly, teasingly simple. Ask.

This is how Jesus himself put it and I suspect that he said it with a twinkle in his eye – even with a laugh. 'If you, being evil (ie bad as you are) know how to give good gifts to your children (and we do; even imprisoned criminals want to give presents to their children at

Christmas), how much more *will* (notice the promise) your Heavenly Father give the Holy Spirit to those who' … are mature Christians? No. … To those who would obtain 90 per cent in a holiness exam? No. '*How much more* (notice the argument) will your Heavenly Father give the Holy Spirit to those who *ask* him.'

Then, when you have asked, *trust* his promise. Here is the promise again: 'How much more *will* your Heavenly Father *give* the Holy Spirit … .'

The stories of *other* people being filled with the Spirit always sound so easy, so effortless, as for example in the story of the man who cried out for wings to carry him up to the nearest tree. That is why I used the word 'teasingly'. When an introvert hears such stories, he may well think to himself, 'How wonderful! Good luck to him! Good luck to her!' Then he adds under his breath, 'But that would never happen to me.' And if you were to ask 'why?', he would reply, 'Because I'm not that type. I'm an introvert. I'm not given to flights of emotion.'

Now you may suspect that he is deceiving himself and that the true answer is rank unbelief of which he will have to repent. Nevertheless, a new step of faith can be difficult for all of us. Faith drags us out of our comfort zones. Doubts and fears assail us – especially, 'What will our friends think? Am I going over the top?' Jesus anticipated this. He could not have been more encouraging. He had just said, 'Ask, and you will receive. Seek, and you will find. Knock, and it will be opened to you.' Then, as if he knows that we may find this no picnic, he puts it round the other way, 'For everyone who asks, receives. Everyone who seeks, finds. And to everyone who knocks, it will be opened.' (Not, by the way, everyone *except* a phlegmatic introvert with a proper distaste for emotionalism.) Six times, Jesus says, 'Go on asking, go on knocking at the door of heaven, and it will happen. The Holy Spirit will be given.'

Mind you, we may have to persevere. Bishop Alfred Stanway used to say, 'If you see something in the Christian life in glorious Technicolor, don't be fobbed off with black and white.' It is no good saying, 'I once spent a few minutes praying that God would fill me with his Spirit and nothing happened.' 'Nothing happened' is one of the devil's lies by means of which he robs us of God's promised blessings. I don't know why God sometimes delays. It may be that he wants to speak to us about weaknesses in our character of which we are unaware. He may see that our faith needs some remedial exercises to toughen it up before he can answer our prayer. But go on asking, go on repenting, go on praising him for all he has done in your life already. Never allow the expectation of future blessings to rob you of your present joy in him. Go on making him 'Lord of all' in so far as you understand at the time. Above all, go on trusting the promise, 'He will give.'

It will happen.

So don't be afraid to abandon yourself to the God who made you, who loves you, who sent his Son to die for you, and is longing to fill you with the Spirit of Jesus. In order that you might be like him (by the *grace* of the Spirit) and do what he did (by the *gifts* of the Spirit).

I say again, 'Don't be afraid'. People in love have many ways of expressing their love for each other. Two especially: a word and a kiss. God's word to me, reduced to a proton is, 'I love you.' His Spirit is his kiss. To be filled with the Holy Spirit is simply allowing yourself to be kissed by God. Being in the arms of the Holy Trinity is a safe and happy place.

The next page should be a 'Believing page'. But before we come to that, I would like, if I can, to clear up two problems that cripple some Christians.

The first is this. If you have had contact with the occult world – Ouija boards, séances, tarot cards, table rapping and such like; or if you have been deeply hurt and are finding it impossible to forgive, you must stop. Faced with the occult and unforgiveness, the wind of the Spirit dies away. These two things are a serious blockage. You will need to draw on the help of experienced Christians whom you like and trust. Be humble. Don't be afraid to tell them exactly what happened. Let them pray with you and for you. This is always a blessing. It is the way in which these blockages are removed.

Then, again, some thoughtful Christians are jittery about praying to the Holy Spirit. They say, rightly, 'I know that the Holy Spirit is *in* me; I know that I belong to Jesus. How, then, can I ask him to come to me?'[12]

To this difficulty, I would again gladly bring a little ease, if I can. Let me quote Professor Gordon Fee.[13]

> Paul had none of our hang-ups over whether a Christian [a person who belongs to Jesus] can 'receive the Spirit' ... . He could not imagine the Spirit in static terms. Hence, he can speak of believers being 'given' the Spirit (1 Thessalonians 4:8) or being 'supplied' with the Spirit (Gal. 3:5) ... For Paul the resident Spirit is ever being given, or 'supplied' anew in the individual believer's or community's life.

'Go on being filled with the Spirit', Paul wrote.[14] He also knew his own need of the Spirit in a *fresh* way, if 'Christ were to be magnified in him' while he was in prison.

In our weakness and inability to do the tasks that God has given us, it is always right for us to pray, 'Come, Holy Spirit.' We have his promise. 'How much more will he give the Holy Spirit to those who ask him.' So we can ask with confidence. We will then experience new and enriching 'fillings'. Indeed, God may surprise us. The little blue pilot light may suddenly blaze up with a roar, and warm the whole house.

I hope that this short explanation will enable us to turn to the next section with confidence.

## *Believing pages*

A promise: Jesus said, 'If anyone thirst, let him come to me and drink. Whoever believes in me, out of his heart shall flow rivers of living water.'

## *Some questions*

Do you believe that anyone includes you?

Are you thirsty? (see p. 126).

Is Christ your Lord? Lord of all?

Do you believe that God will keep his promise – and that the Holy Spirit will fill you, and flow out from you?

A further promise: 'How much more will your Father in heaven give the Holy Spirit to those who ask him' (Luke 11:13).

## *So, ask him*

*Come Holy Spirit. Come!*
*Come as the fire – to burn up sin.*
*Come as oil – to heal.*

*Come as the water – to refresh, and to flow out in blessing.*
*Come as the wind – to empower me for your glorious service.*
*Come to do – what today needs to be done in my life.*
*Come and fill me.*
*Come Holy Spirit. Come! Amen.*

Next: Read the promise again. Trust the promise. Tell God, in your own words, that you are resting on the word 'will'. Better still, 'pass through' the promise and embrace your Heavenly Father. Praise him for his love and generosity. Tell him that you trust him.

Next: Pray the prayer again, this time turning it into praise. 'Dear Holy Spirit, thank you for coming to me. Thank you for coming to me as fire … . Thank you for coming to me as water …' and so on. The prayer then expresses and strengthens your faith. Don't worry about feelings.

# *Notes*

1. Charles Wesley, in his hymn, 'O thou who camest from above'.
2. See 1 Samuel 9:1ff. Some donkeys wander off (4). Saul searches for them uphill and down dale, but can't find them. He wants to go home (5), but his servant suggests that they visit Samuel. The servant just happens to have a silver coin to pay the prophet's fee. Some girls tell them the way (11), and say that they have arrived at the right moment. They ask a man to direct them to Samuel (18), and the man turns out to be Samuel himself. It all seems so ordinary – a day 'down at the farm'. And yet twelve hours before, God had told Samuel in great detail exactly what was going to happen. 'Tomorrow ... *I* will send you a man' (9:16ff, my italics).
3. From 'O Little Town of Bethlehem'.
4. Such richly blessed Christians need to grasp, as quickly as possible, how the cross of Jesus fits in, and why the cross was necessary. (See Events 1 and 2 of the diagram.) Their spiritual experience cries out to be earthed in God's words and God's promises. Then if, for whatever reason, the glory begins to fade, they are safe. They *understand* what Christ has done for them.
5. 1 Corinthians 14:2, 4.
6. John 7:37–39, RSV.
7. From 'When I Survey the Wondrous Cross' by Isaac Watts (italics mine).
8. Nicky Gumbel, *Questions of Life* (Alpha International, 2010), p.245.
9. Richard Foster, *Simplicity*, p.102.
10. Sheldon Vanauken, *A Severe Mercy* (Hodder & Stoughton, 2011), p.94.
11. Malcolm Muggeridge, *Jesus Rediscovered* (Fontana Books), 1970, p.100.
12. Romans 8:9: 'If anyone does not have the Spirit of Christ, he does not belong to Christ' (my italics), clearly implying that if we belong to Christ we *have* the Holy Spirit.
13. Gordon Fee, *God's Empowering Presence* (Hendricksons Publishers, 1994), pp.741–42.
14. Ephesians 5:18; my translation of the Greek, retaining the sense of 'continuous filling'.

*Chapter 6*

# The Gifts of the Spirit

The gifts of the Spirit are a huge, but neglected, subject. Many of them are mentioned in the Bible. In the Old Testament there is a sparkling display of them in the lives of the leaders and the prophets: healings and great miracles, but also kindly, trivial ones, like helping to find some lost sheep or a borrowed axe. Trivial, we may feel, but of no little importance to their owners. Have you not read these stories, and thought to yourself, 'Oh, I wish that some of these things would happen to me – with missing spectacles and lost car keys'? Well, in those far off days they did happen, not because these leaders were psychic, but for *one* reason only. They were filled with the Holy Spirit.

Then again, Prophecy, with her flickering lamp, threads her way through the darkness of the Old Testament, giving us astonishing glimpses of what was to come. The prophet Daniel mentions an anointed prince. There is only one person who fits this description: Jesus – anointed with what? The Holy

Spirit. Another prophet, Joel, looked forward to a time when God would pour out the Spirit, not simply on a few lucky Jewish leaders, but upon *all* mankind – that is, upon anybody open to receive the Spirit of Jesus. By Pentecost, the Prince of the Spirit had come, the people of the Spirit had come; and until Jesus returns to the world at his second coming, we are living in a final age, the age of the Spirit. So it is not surprising that, in the early church, there was another dazzling display of the gifts of the Spirit. These were never given to puff up the disciples, or to grab the limelight, or for selfish purposes. They seem rather to have been prompted by sheer compassion (especially the healing gifts) – a sense that 'something must be done'.

In one of his lists of the gifts of the Spirit, St Paul mentions the 'message of knowledge'.[1] To some Christians, he says, the Spirit manifests himself by giving them such a message of knowledge;[2] or, as we might say, 'The Spirit shows himself by speaking, and by telling us something that only he knows.'

Now what I find so fascinating is this. We know from several stories in the Acts of the Apostles that the Holy Spirit has a voice. For example, when Philip was in the desert on the road to Gaza, he saw a carriage bumping along with a man in it. The man was reading. At that moment, the Spirit spoke. He *said* to Philip, 'Go and join that carriage.'[3] Philip listened and obeyed. Indeed, he ran. The stranger, a distinguished Ethiopian, invited him to climb up and sit with him.

Philip then discovered to his astonishment that, in the scroll, by God's miraculous timing, he had just reached the best paragraph in Isaiah for explaining why it was necessary for Jesus to be crucified. The consequences were far-reaching. Not only did the Ethiopian become a Christian, get baptised and go on his way rejoicing, but this seems to have been God's plan for taking the gospel to Africa. So we have a pattern here: the Spirit speaks, a Christian listens and obeys, and profound consequences follow.[4]

Two questions naturally arise. First, does the Spirit speak from the sky? This is best answered by asking another question, 'Where was the Holy Spirit on the road to Gaza?' And the answer, of course, is that he was 'in' Philip. So when I am asked 'How does the Spirit speak? Does he speak through a good thought? Or through a picture? (Do you *see* the lost keys or whatever?) Or through a message that comes so clearly to mind that it *seems* to come from outside?' I reply that it may be any one of these: but that, in this gift, the Holy Spirit uses our brains, whereas in a language for praise or prayer given by the Spirit, he uses our lips.

The second question is this: 'Does the Spirit still wish to speak to us today?' To this question I would answer a resounding 'Yes'. Even if Philip and Peter had known the Old Testament scriptures by heart, there was nothing in *them* to lead Philip to hitchhike on a particular carriage, or to coax Peter to descend from his roof top, and set off on a thirty mile trek with three strangers ('Gentile dogs', to boot).[5] In both stories the Spirit spoke. In fact, God has always shown an intense desire to communicate with us, sometimes on matters of importance to him, but often, too, simply because he loves us, and because he sees that there is an immediacy in our situation that cries out for his special help.

At the height of 'the troubles' in Northern Ireland, there was a Christian woman who kept a small shop. One Saturday evening, she locked the front door and went into the back room to count her takings for the week. She was halfway through when the Spirit spoke to her. He said, 'Put the money away.' She didn't recognise the whisper of the Spirit, and took no notice. The Spirit spoke again with greater urgency, 'Put the money away.' This time she was alarmed. She threw the money into a box, and put the box behind a cushion on the sofa. At that moment, there was a crash at the back of the house, followed by heavy footsteps in the passage, and two hooded men burst into the room. They threw the woman on to the sofa. They then ransacked the room, looking for the week's money. They found nothing. She was sitting on it. Here was the Holy Spirit protecting one of God's children in danger, and I am reminded of the Israeli-Syrian war of 2 Kings 6:8. The King of Israel had escaped the ambushes set for him by the King of Syria so regularly that the King of Syria thought that there must be a leak. Eventually he discovered that the prophet Elisha was

Israel's secret weapon. The Holy Spirit told Elisha the Syrian campaign secrets, and he passed them on to the King of Israel. These were 'messages of knowledge'.[6]

People often imagine that gifts of the Spirit are only of interest in the context of church matters. Not so; they can be concerned with political and military matters of national importance.[7] In 587 BC, when Jerusalem was destroyed, some army officers and a sizeable group of men and women went to Jeremiah and asked him whether they should stay in Judea or migrate to Egypt. They were not interested in God's plans; simply in their own safety. Common sense said, 'Get out while you can.' Jeremiah retired for ten days. After ten days, God spoke. They must stay. Nevertheless they went.

A Russian prophet, Efim, born about 1842, and who lived in Kara Kala, a village in South Armenia, gave a prophetic word that included a number of words of knowledge. It was a warning that sometime in the future every Christian in Armenia would be in great danger. They should leave and go to the west coast of USA where God would bless them. This caused much amusement. Nevertheless some went, including Efim. They prospered. In 1915, the Turks massacred over a million Armenians simply because they were Christians, including all those who still lived in Kara Kala.

It is interesting that these last two stories are examples of disobedience to the prophetic word of God.

Let us sum up where we have reached so far. You may remember that I said, in Event 3, that God speaks to us chiefly through the Bible. We must never forget that. But I hope that you are also beginning to be persuaded that God loves to communicate with us by his Spirit, and I now want to make this thrilling truth stand out in bold relief.

Perhaps you are thinking, 'Why do I not hear his voice more often?' The answer may be simple: it may be that he *is* speaking, and that you are not recognising his whispers. That was my problem; and only after making many mistakes did I begin to realise that 'a good thought' was, perhaps, the common or garden way in which he spoke, and that I needed to be sensitive to these good thoughts, and to act on them *promptly* – not in three weeks' time, if I still felt like it. I remember asking a friend whom I admired, 'How does one know when the Spirit is speaking?' She replied somewhat sharply, 'Can't you recognise your mother's voice?' She was right to rebuke me. I was being slow. Philip in the desert received a clearly spelt-out message, 'Go and join that carriage.' For us the Spirit may decide that a hint, a nudge, should be sufficient. But I can promise that, if you follow up these hints, you will discover that 'God writes extraordinary novels in the lives of those of us who are open to the unexpected, and on the alert to hear the whispers of the Spirit.'[8]

A further reason is that the Spirit finds us hard of hearing in the twenty-first century. We are in such a hurry. Until the early nineteenth century, many long-case clocks had only an hour hand. What did thirty minutes matter? Now – such is the pace of life – people are upset if they have to wait for the next section of a revolving door. Then there is the ubiquity of noise – a tragedy of our age. Jesus climbed mountains to be quiet. Philip was in the silence of the desert when the Spirit spoke. If they ever climb a mountain, some people take care to carry an iPod, spewing out now musac, now newzac, to avoid boring silences.

However, nothing is too hard for the Lord! So, stand by for a story. Gerald was a Christian. One day a friend said to him, 'In your prayers, you shouldn't spend all the available time talking. Give God time to speak.'

Gerald filed this thought away in his mind and eventually decided to try it out. He wrote afterwards: 'As soon as my mind had cleared, I was shocked by the sudden awareness that Jesus was present. I couldn't see him. But I knew that he was there, that he was holding out his arms towards me and was saying, "Come to me." Again, these words surprised me. They implied that I was some distance from him, whereas I had been quite content with my relationship with him. Indeed, I felt that he should be rather happy to have me as his disciple. So I said, "I love you, Lord. What more do you want me to do?" At once, I realised that my attitude was wrong. I fell at his feet. He began to speak… .'[9]

I am not suggesting that every time we sit quietly in God's presence we shall have a similarly dramatic interview with him. Jeremiah had to withdraw for ten days before the Spirit spoke. But let us make it our firm aim to give God time to speak to us. We have his promise: 'Draw near to God, and he will draw near to you.'[10] He wants us to enjoy this enthralling privilege. It may be just a whisper. But it may be more. We may be surprised.

So far I have been thinking about the Spirit speaking to the individual: to Philip, to a shopkeeper in Northern Ireland, and to Gerald. But in New Testament days he clearly loved to speak to *groups* of worshipping Christians. Writing to the Corinthian church, St Paul said, 'When you come together, *everyone* of you has … a revelation' (probably a term that covers both words of knowledge and prophecy). In addition, he particularly recommended us to desire prophecy. Of course! Because we then have the opportunity of becoming God's spokesperson, and what an extraordinary honour this is.

In one of the churches I served, there were a dozen or so members of the congregation who took on a special responsibility. They agreed to come to church an hour before the evening service, wait upon God in prayer and see whether the Spirit would graciously speak to them. They would then discuss any word of knowledge or 'picture' that had been given; if they agreed that the message had been rightly heard, they would write it down and pass the piece of paper to whoever was leading the service.

One evening, I was leading the service. I was handed a slip of paper that read, 'There is somebody here with a swollen and painful ankle. If they come forward for prayer at the end of the service, they will be healed.' Now, it was a big congregation, and I was conscious that there were at least three distinguished doctors who were present. Would they not say, 'This is trivial stuff?' After all, the best thing to do with a strained ankle is to rest it. So I hesitated. There was no hurry and, as the service continued, I prayed. I felt peace of heart; I also trusted the team. So I took a deep breath and read out the message.

A girl came forward. Her name was Kiran. She was a school teacher. She was Indian and Hindu; a friend had invited her to this church. As she had run down the steps of her flat the day before, her ankle had turned over and it had been painful and swollen ever since. So when she heard the message given out, she said to herself, 'This is for me.' Two people prayed that Jesus would heal her, laying their hands on her ankle. Immediately the pain went. She was deeply impressed. Not only had she been healed, but she now knew that Jesus was alive and had healed her. She became a Christian.

Kiran's brother was an undergraduate at Cambridge, studying medicine. She wrote to him and told him what had happened. He began to attend services, whenever he could. He introduced himself to one of my colleagues and, after much vigorous debate, he, too, became a Christian. After some months, I went to a small party that we were holding for newcomers to the church. Among the guests was a striking Indian lady, swathed in a sari. 'What brings you here?,' I asked. 'I have come', she replied, 'to see what you have done to my son. I haven't heard him laugh for three years, and now I can't stop him.' She, too, became a Christian. After instruction, all three were baptised. So you see that a word of knowledge about a swollen ankle, apparently trivial, was the first link in a chain of events by which the Holy Spirit drew these three into God's kingdom. I am thankful that I gave out the message.

By the way, I don't think we need be worried by people who say, 'Surely you will soon be plagued with crazy, silly messages.' This has not been my experience. In many churches, there are *naturally* gifted men and women, and when these men and women are surrendered to the Lord, what a blessing they can be as they use their gifts of cooking, cleaning, accountancy, music, and countless other gifts, to serve him. The oil of the Spirit makes all the difference. But we can go a step further. There can also be *spiritually* gifted men and women, full of faith and compassion, carefully selected and appointed to wait on God together, as they did in the church at Antioch. Such a group, always under the authority of the leader(s), can have a profound influence on the life and direction of a church. This is a whole new ball game. At Antioch, for example, it led directly to Paul's first missionary journey, and eventually to Christianity spreading over Europe. I would add that there is a safeguard from wild ideas when a sensible, and carefully selected group, is prepared to take part in a sacrificial and time-devouring ministry. (Of course, if dear, unhinged souls are appointed, the church will get what it deserves!)

Here I stop. I only hope that I have said enough to whet your appetite. It is a wonderful theme. I have said a little about one gift, the word of knowledge, and touched on another, prophecy, for they often overlap. But there are many more. And, as I said earlier, it is a neglected theme. Paul has nine in one of his lists.[11] When did you last hear a talk on the gift of faith? Or on miracles? (Not on whether they ever happen, but how we can help to create the atmosphere of faith and expectancy in which Jesus is able to do his mighty works.) Or on the gift of the single life?! Perhaps the time will come when such talks become commonplace, and we begin to see, in the churches, not only all the graces of the Spirit, but also all the gifts of the Spirit. Then the life of the church will remind the world of Jesus. There will be a fairy story quality about it. His body will have returned to health.

As the following is the first page in the book on which you will see the complete diagram (Events 1 to 5), I cannot resist drawing your attention to a remarkable prophecy. As you know, there were three important Jewish festivals, instituted by God well over 1,000 years earlier, on which important events in the gospel story took place: (i) Passover (the cross – Event 1); (ii) the first fruits that took place three days later (the resurrection – Event 3); (iii) Pentecost or the Harvest/Tabernacles that

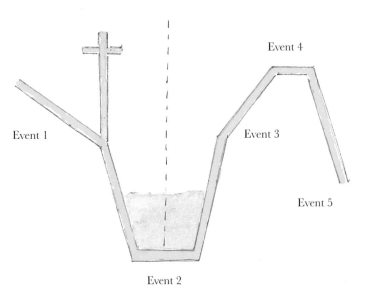

Event 4

Event 1

Event 3

Event 5

Event 2

took place fifty days after the first fruits (the pouring out of the Holy Spirit – Event 5).

Now, look at the timing!

(i) God *chose* the date of the cross despite all human efforts to avoid the Passover festival (Then the chief priests and the elders of the people took counsel together in order to arrest Jesus by stealth and to kill him. But they said, '*Not* during the feast lest there be a tumult among the people.' Matthew 26:3ff).

(ii) God *chose* the date of the resurrection (the day after the Passover Sabbath or Easter Saturday). 'Christ the first fruits of those who have fallen asleep (or died)' (1 Corinthians 15:20).

(iii) God *chose* the moment when he poured out the Holy Spirit – at Pentecost, the first harvest of men and women of the Gospel Age. Do you think that this was part of the Bible study that Jesus gave to the two disciples on the road to Emmaus?

# *Notes*

1. Unfortunately for us, the Apostle does not describe the gifts. He assumes that we know what they are. In the context, he is pointing out that the human body has *many* parts, yet there is only *one* body (ie there is variety within the unity). So it with the gifts of the Spirit – there are *many* gifts but only *one* Holy Spirit.

2. In Greek the phrase 'the message of' means either 'a message' or 'the act of uttering'.

3. Acts 8:29.

4. You will find the same pattern in the story of Peter and Cornelius (Acts 10:19) and in Paul and Barnabas at Antioch (Acts 13:2). Both were major turning points in the spread of Christianity.

5. Acts 10:9ff. The attitude of the Jews to the heathen may seem harsh to us. But in their long Old Testament history, they struggled to be God's holy nation, and they were afraid, with good reason, of being corrupted by close contact with the surrounding nations. St John touches on this in John 4:9.

6. Translated 'The word of knowledge' in the Authorized Version.

7. General Montgomery was reading the first lesson in his village church. It was from Deuteronomy, and was the story of God briefing Moses with the correct strategy for a battle. He began to read, 'The Lord said unto Moses … .' Here he paused, took off his glasses, looked round the congregation and said, 'And in *my* judgment, He was *absolutely* right!'

8. Cardinal Suenens, *A New Pentecost?* (Darton, 1975), p.66.

9. Professor Bruce Yocum, *Prophecy* (Servant Publications, 1976).

10. James 4:8 (RSV).

11. I recommend Alison Morgan, *Doing What Jesus Did*, ReSource, 2009. This is a scholarly, but practical, introduction to the gifts of the Spirit, and contains many real-life stories.

*Chapter 7*

# Sacraments

You may be surprised that, apart from a brief mention in chapter 3, I have said nothing about the sacraments. Christians have differed as to whether they should believe in two sacraments, seven, or even thousands; but all Christians are agreed on the unique significance of the two given to us by Jesus himself: baptism and the Holy Communion (or the Lord's Supper, as it is called in the New Testament, or the Eucharist, or the Mass as it became known in the medieval church). To show you that these two sacraments have never been far from my mind, I invite you to look at the completed diagram on the opposite page and to put a circle round it. If we then fill up the gulf with blue water, we have the first sacrament, the doctrine of baptism.

Can you decipher this for yourself? Before reading on, it might be good to pause, look at the completed diagram, and see whether you can spell out *how* the *water* of baptism illumines Event 1. (Is that double

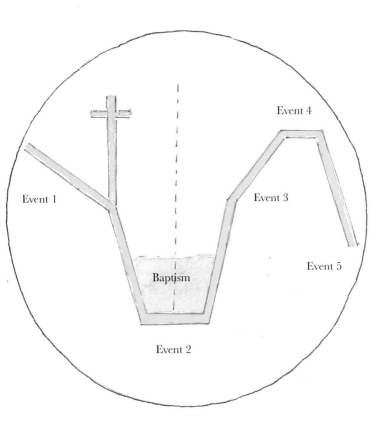

Dutch? Should I add, 'I trust I make myself obscure'? Well, be patient! In time, all will be revealed.)

I suspect that you will solve one, and you might be able to manage five. What about the rest? Two is very hard unless you happen to know that Jesus once called his crucifixion a baptism. 'I have a baptism to undergo,' he said, 'and how distressed I am until it is completed' (Luke 12:50). He seems to have used the word because water not only washes, it drowns. There is, therefore, a streak of violence in the word 'baptism'. In the Greek language, if a ship had been 'baptised', it was sunk – it had gone to the bottom! You might now be able to solve two. Nobody could guess three and four. So let me explain. Peter was a fisherman. He understood the sea. He seems to have liked the story of the flood, and of the great boat that God had told Noah to build to rescue his family and the animals. He mentions Noah in both his letters, and he links the ark with baptism.[1] With those clues, let us look at the completed diagram again.

What I was fishing for was something like this. In Christ, the dirt of sin is washed away – Event 1. In Christ, I share his crucifixion (a baptism) and I share his death and burial. Indeed, baptism marks the funeral, the full stop, of all that I was in Adam before I became a Christian – Event 2. In Christ, like Noah and the animals in the ark, I am brought safely through God's just judgment on a sinful world to the risen and ascended life – Events 3 and 4. In Christ, I experience, and continue to experience, the rushing waters of the empowering Holy Spirit – Event 5.

You can see how well all this is dramatised when new Christians are baptised in a river – as they often are in hot climates.

Notice, too, that the movement of the sacrament is downward: from heaven to earth. It is all *God's* grace; all *God's* action. We don't baptise ourselves. The baptiser represents Christ. Mind you, there must always be faith somewhere: the faith of the person being baptised, the faith of the parents, and perhaps the faith of those who are welcoming the candidate into the Christian family. 'Without faith it is impossible to please God'.[2] Without faith in Christ and in what he has achieved, even in a perfectly ordered baptism service, we will go down into the water dry sinners, and come up wet sinners.

I will share a dark secret with you. I would love to have been baptised four times or more. I was baptised as a baby. This, in my judgment, was right because I had the immense privilege of being born into a Christian family.[3] My parents knew about Abraham, and how God had told him to circumcise his son when he was a baby: a sign that God had promised that he would love little Isaac, be with little Isaac and reveal himself to little Isaac as he grew up. My father and mother reasoned that, although the sign had changed from circumcision (suitable for a Jewish boy) to water (suitable for boys and girls the world over), God's promises remain the same. I know that they often claimed those promises for me in their prayers. Then when I was eighteen, I came to know Christ personally. The Christian life came alive. I would love to have been baptised then; a second time. Many years later, I discovered Romans chapter 6. That would have been the third. Finally, to my astonishment and surprise, I have been filled, or rather drenched, with the Spirit once or twice. Those could have been baptisms number four and five! I say 'to my astonishment', because I was not expecting such blessings, and I certainly didn't deserve them: rather the reverse. Simply, I believe, God saw that without special strengthening, I was so desperate, so weak and scared, that I would be unable to do what he wanted me to do. In Romans 6, Paul does not tell the Christians at Rome to be re-baptised. He writes in astonishment, 'Don't you know ...?' Don't you know what your baptism *means*? So I like the phrase *going deeper into* your baptism. At each of these mountaintop experiences, I *went deeper* into *my* baptism. That is to say, I became, thankfully, less ignorant of the meaning of this rich and wonderful sacrament; and more aware that it is always God who takes the first kind step towards me. From heaven to earth.

But we can go further. As I said in the introduction, these five doctrines underpin the whole of the Christian life. They also, therefore, apply to the Holy Communion.

Let me put it like this. When we reach the heart of the Holy Communion service, we watch the bread being broken. We see the cup being held up. We wait. We walk forward. We eat the bread. We drink the wine. We return to our seats. What are we thinking about?

I have argued, at length on p. 77, that there should be something of a *party* atmosphere, a *fun* atmosphere, about our Christian lives – something that mirrors those evening parties attended by Jesus in the Gospel stories. They must have been so enjoyable and so stimulating that his disciples tried never to miss a 'Lord's Supper'. Another beautiful name that the first Christians coined for it in the second century was 'the Eucharist' or, 'the Thanksgiving'. This, presumably, was because, with good food, good wine, close friends, healings, miracles and other gifts of the Spirit flowing from the loving presence of the risen Lord, the characteristic features of these gatherings were adoring worship, joy, thanksgiving, and tears of gratitude.

Richard Wurnbrandt was a Romanian Pastor of outstanding presence, courage, intelligence and wit, who spent fourteen years in prison behind the Communist iron curtain. During those years, he was starved, tortured, and suffered long periods of solitary confinement. In 1970 he was allowed to escape to England after a ransom had been paid. At that time I was linked with a school of Christian foundation, which, in those days, like many schools of that tradition, held services in chapel three times a week. The boys and girls were expected to be present. Richard came to preach. After the service, I took him across to a hall where the school had gathered for a question and answer session. A small boy stood up and asked in a miserable voice, 'Sir, do you believe in compulsory chapel?' There was a long silence. The headmaster and housemasters looked anxious. What would this visitor say? Would he undermine the discipline of the school? Wurnbrandt contemplated the small boy gravely: 'Are you actually telling me that you *have* to attend these services?' 'Yes,

Sir,' said the small boy, even more miserably. Then Wurnbrandt said, 'Do you *run* to chapel?' 'Not usually, Sir.' Wurnbrandt looked puzzled. 'You don't *run*! Why, why do you not *run*?' The conversation had taken an unexpected turn, and the small boy was clearly out of his depth. 'In Romania,' Wurnbrandt continued, 'sadly the churches are closed and locked. But if they were open, we would *run* to worship in them. We would be so, so thankful for our freedom. Do you not realise? In chapel,[4] God the Father, God the Son, God the Holy Spirit, crowds of angels, and the church in heaven and earth are waiting to welcome you. Why do you not *run*?' There was no reply – just a sigh of relief from the headmaster and staff.

Now, keeping this theme of thanksgiving in mind, and returning to my question, 'What are we thinking about at the heart of the service?' Here are some possible answers and a plan of action.[5] George Herbert wrote:

A man who looks on glass,
On it may stay his eye;
Or, if he pleaseth, through it, *pass*
And then the heaven espy.[6]

First, with the eye of faith, we must '*pass through*' the outward forms of the bread and the wine, and 'espy', or see, the heavenly world. We espy the Lord himself. He is about to minister to us. He is 'the bread of life' and he promised us that those who eat that bread would 'never hunger'. How, then, do we 'eat'? Well, he tells us: by coming to him (in prayer), and by believing in him. So this is where we begin. We express our love and trust in him, *especially* if we are feeling battered by life. Perhaps we whisper, 'Lord, it's been a bad week; everything seems to have gone wrong; it's a dark night, with no moon or stars. *But* I trust you.' In our hearts we bow before him, worship him, and *thank* him for being with us. We espy the angels all round him. And all round us.

Then our turn comes to go forward to the Communion rail. And now we see the *broken* bread, and the wine poured out. We remember that Jesus died for us, the Lamb of God, bearing away the sin of the world. We murmur 'Jesus, who loved *me*, and gave himself for *me*' and, in our own words, we *thank* him that we are totally forgiven. We also remember that he took us *in* him to the cross, that, in him, the old John, the old Jane, died and was buried; and that now, risen with Christ, we have crossed the gulf to newness of life. We are equipped to fight the devil and *to win*. Again, we pour out our hearts in love and *thanksgiving*. Thus, as we eat and drink, we feast, by faith, on Christ crucified.

When we rise from our knees at the Communion rail, and open our eyes, we see, all round us, other members of the Christian family. We *thank* God for their kindness, friendship and encouragement. We remember how close we are to them in Christ; like the loaf before it is broken. Writing about the bread at the Lord's Supper, St Paul said, 'We, many as we are, are *one* loaf, *one* body. For we all share in the *one* loaf.' This is another way of thinking of the piece of bread that is placed in our hands. It represents myself. The person kneeling next to me also has a piece of bread. It represents her. Both pieces come from the *one* loaf. (We don't, of course *become* one by eating the bread. We *become* part of the one body of Christ by trusting in Christ crucified and risen, and by receiving his Spirit.) Nevertheless we declare our oneness and solidarity with the Christians round about us. So we think to ourselves, 'To whom can I show God's love? Is there anyone whom I should forgive? Should I say to anyone, '"I'm sorry that I upset you?"'

Forgiveness, you know, is a matter of the will. 'I will never forgive him,' people say. They are often full of bitterness. Note well, they have made a choice. They have *chosen* not to forgive. But, of course, with God's help, we can do exactly the opposite. We can *choose* to forgive.[7]

As we return to our seat, and sit down, we remember that we are 'sitting with' Christ, in the heavenly world, sharing his throne. Again, we pour out our prayers and *thanksgiving*. Finally, we ask our heavenly Father to fill us with the Holy Spirit, plant our faith securely on his promise, and *thank* him for answering our prayer. We have now discovered five great reasons for *giving thanks to God* at the Holy Communion.

Perhaps you say, 'Have I got to think of all this every time I take the bread and the wine?' Not if you don't feel like it! In 1818, Jean-Baptiste Vianney became the Curé d'Ars, or, as we would say in England, the Vicar of Ars, a lonely village some distance from Lyons. There was an old farm labourer living there. His name was Chaffangeon. He used to come to the empty church nearly every day and, after kneeling to say the Lord's Prayer, would sit quietly in the pew for hours at a time, gazing at the picture of Christ crucified, in the east window. So, one day, the Curé said to him, 'M'sieur, I see you sitting here so often. I can't help wondering what it going on in your mind?' 'Going on in my mind, M'sieur le Curé?' said the old man with a smile: 'Nothing much. I am no good at thinking.' Then, after a pause, he pointed to the figure of Jesus in the window, and said slowly, 'He looks at me. I look at him. And we are happy.' What could be more lovely? He was basking in the sunshine of the presence of the Lord. He would have been confused, at a deep level, by my diagram. He probably had never heard of the doctrine of justification by grace and faith. But, like Brother Lawrence, he was enjoying the fruit of that amazing doctrine Event 1. He had been hungry for God, hungry for righteousness. Jesus, who sees all hearts, had loved him and come to him.

When we are tired, just to 'espy' the Lord, as George Herbert wrote, and to be with him, and with his family, will be enough. Nevertheless, Jesus has invited us to take part in this wonderful and mysterious sacrament. Indeed, he has commanded us 'to do this, until he comes again'. We must therefore struggle to understand what he had in mind.

The story of Chaffangeon leads me to say one thing more. Justification leaps over the centuries to the last day, the day of judgment, the day when the Lord returns in glory. It assures me that, if tomorrow I am run over by an Oxford City bus, all is well. John Bunyan put it like this. 'Now I saw in my dream that these two men [Christian and Faithful] went in at the gate [of the Celestial City]; and lo, as they entered, they were transfigured, and they had raiment put on that shone like gold. Then I heard in my dream that all the bells in the City rang again for joy, and that it was said unto them, "Enter ye into the joy of your Lord."'[8] So we *feast* together on bread and *wine* (not bread and water), looking forward eagerly to that great reunion when we will meet Jesus face to face, inherit the kingdom prepared for us and *feast* together. Then all heaven will be let loose.

In the meantime, if I can escape the Oxford City bus for a few more years, there is much to be done.

# *Notes*

1. 'In the days of Noah, during the building of the ark, in which a few, that is, eight persons, were saved through water. Baptism, which corresponds to this …' (1 Peter 3:20–21).

2. Hebrews 11:6.

3. If children, baptised as infants, grow up and find that their parents show no interest in Christianity, a convincing argument can be made for some form of 'making good' their baptism. Many bishops accept this.

4. The same, of course, would be true if we were worshipping together in the open air.

5. I am a member of the Church of England; but with slight modification, I think that what I am saying can easily be adjusted to the practice of other denominations.

6. From 'Teach Me, My God and King'.

7. If forgiveness is a problem, and it seems very hard when we have been badly hurt, read Matthew 18: 21–35, and get help.

8. John Bunyan, *The Pilgrim's Progress*, 1678. The definitive text was produced in 1826 by the Religious Tract Society, taking into account Bunyan's final revision – the rare 11th edition in 1688 – shortly before he died. In modern editions, this quotation will be found in the final two or three pages of the book.

*Chapter 8*

# Things Hard to
# Understand: Part 1

When I wrote about Romans 6 in chapter 2, the second Event in the diagram, it is possible that some well-instructed readers were puzzled, even dismayed. They might think to themselves, 'This is clear and simple and oh! how wonderful if it is true.' And then they start thinking, 'Surely this explanation is flatly contradicted by the struggle between "the flesh and the Spirit" in Galatians 5:16–17, and by the inner war of "the wretched man" described in Romans 7.' As they read these two passages again, their spirits sink. Reluctantly, they come to the conclusion that, alas, this exhilarating new vision from Romans *can't* be true, and that they will have to continue to shuffle along, monkey and all, until everything is put right in heaven.

It is only fair, therefore, to look at these two passages – Galatians in this chapter, and Romans in chapter 9 and try to understand what St Paul may be saying. And now a confession. Despite my affection for the acronym KISS,[1] I have had to look at verses that bristle with difficulties. There are many maps laying a claim to guide Christian pilgrims through Romans 7, but whichever road they take, they are soon faced with the notice 'Here be dragons'. I have therefore chosen one route out of many, a road recommended as safe by some great students of the New Testament: although certainly not by all. There is no final agreement. I feel that I should tell you that these two chapters are somewhat specialist. If you suspect that they are not your concern, I fully understand. Skip them with a clear conscience and rejoin the diagram on p. 201.

During the last fifty years, through the painstaking labours of scholars, I am delighted to say that fresh light has shone from them. Let me try to explain, beginning with Galatians.

According to one popular translation, this is what St Paul wrote. 'So I say, live by the Spirit, and you will not gratify the desires of the sinful nature. For the sinful nature desires what is contrary to the Spirit, and the Spirit what is contrary to the sinful nature. They are in conflict with each other, so that you do not do what you want.'[2] Then follows an ugly list of the acts of 'the sinful nature' and, contrasted with it, a beautiful list of the fruit of the Spirit. If this translation is correct, the meaning seems to be plain. In every Christian a civil war is raging. First, inside us, is 'the sinful nature' that has been inherited from birth. But also, in us, is the

Holy Spirit; and, as the apostle points out, these 'are in conflict'. How could they not be if one is holy and the other is sinful? As a Christian, I have to admit that sometimes it *feels* like that: though, of course, we would also have to admit that *feelings* are an unreliable yardstick for the true state of affairs in the Christian life. They often deceive us; especially when we remember that the devil has access to our thoughts, and that therefore what *seems* to come from inside may, like the 'flaming arrows' of Ephesians chapter 6,[3] actually come from outside.

But then, at the end of the quotation, there follows a sad admission: 'so that [ie as a consequence of the civil war] you do not do what you want.'[4] That is, you don't carry out the desires of the Spirit *because of* the strong opposition of the flesh. Here is a recent comment on this tension between flesh and Spirit that I have just described. 'In consequence the believer finds himself torn in two by conflicting desires and impulses, and his experience as a man of the Spirit in the flesh is one of continuing frustration.'[5] I said 'a sad admission,' because is this really all that Christians can hope for in this life? And an enigma, too: for how can we possibly reconcile this sad admission with the confident and joyful cry of Romans 6, 'Sin shall not have dominion over you',[6] let alone with all the other New Testament claims of what Jesus the Saviour makes possible, and in which there is no hint of being 'torn in two', or of 'continuing frustration'.[7] Nevertheless, if the popular translation of Galatians 5:16 and 17 is correct, we must face facts. We are still in the jungle. The monkey is on our back, and there seems to be no escape.

However, it has now become clear that the popular translation (and therefore the popular interpretation) of these two verses is not as secure as thoughtful people once believed. So there may be a gleam of sunlight in the jungle. The experts have been digging away at Galatians chapter 5. They have studied the arguments that come before and after the apostle's 'sad admission', and they point out that there is not a hint that St Paul is exploring *the inner life* of *individual* Christians. On the contrary, in the context, he *is* deeply worried about something quite different, namely, the quality of life in a *Christian community* and, in particular, its lack of love. He was horrified at the bickering and sniping that was taking place in the Galatian churches. 'If you go on chewing each other up,' he says 'there will soon be nothing left.' Stop provoking one another! Stop envying one another!

So he writes to them, 'You *are* set free; but not to do anything you like. You are set free to be love-slaves to one another.' What a startling phrase that is! Faced with a slave and his master, we would assume that only the slave will do any 'slaving'; but in Paul's vision of the Christian community, *both equally* are love-slaves. Of course, the slave will have to slave for his master. (What's the point of having a slave, if he won't do that?) But here the master – of all people – is expected to slave for the slave.

Paul rubs in the lesson with a number of examples. One of them is this. 'Carry one another's luggage,' he says; 'in this way you will fulfil the law of Christ.' So we are treated to a bizarre but beautiful scene from the ancient world. The tired slave walks free. The master humps the luggage. And he does so gladly, because he's a Christian. That is the sort of way the law of love works out in practice. Each illustration Paul offers is the same – nothing to do with exploring the inner life; everything to do with community.

And here is another thing that has alerted the experts. 'Sinful nature' is the translation of a single word in the original – a slippery little word – *sarx*. So in the paragraph in question, wherever 'sinful nature' occurs, the actual word in Greek is *sarx*. And *sarx* has already appeared several times in Paul's letter to the Galatians. Here are two examples. In chapter two, he says, 'I have been crucified with Christ; it is no longer I who live, but Christ who lives in me; and the life I now live *in the flesh (sarx)* I live by faith in the Son of God … .' (RSV). Here the word is entirely neutral, not sinful; indeed, the NIV itself translates it *body*. Then again, in chapter three, Paul reminds his readers that they began their Christian lives by receiving the Spirit, and that God continued the 'rich supply (a generous word)[8] of the Spirit' and it was for that reason they had been experiencing miracles (3:5). Presumably there were extraordinary healings, extraordinary conversions, extraordinary escapes from danger. There was a fairy-story quality about their lives. Why on earth, therefore, he asks, do they want to end up by living *'in the flesh'* (*sarx*)? How foolish! How dull! Again the word seems neutral – simply living an ordinary human life, *but without the Spirit*. St Paul's argument is, 'why return to oil lamps when you can enjoy electric light? Why turn your wine into water?' You may remember that Jesus, in Gethsemane, warned his disciples that *the flesh (sarx)* was weak, and that they needed to pray if they were going to be any use throughout that terrible weekend. Alas, they did what was merely human. They fell asleep, mouths open, quietly snoring: so fragile, so vulnerable, so *weak*. That is exactly how the word is being used in Galatians chapters 2 and 3.

But when we arrive at chapter 5, we are suddenly told by some translators that the meaning of 'flesh' has taken a turn for the worse. No longer neutral, it has spiralled down to 'the *sinful* nature'(NIV) or 'the *lower* nature' (NEB) or 'the *evil* nature' (LIVING BIBLE).[9] There is no word, I assure you, for sinful, lower, or evil in the original. It is simply our weak old friend, '*sarx*'.

We are forced to ask the question, 'Why the change?' Could it be that the translators thought that Romans chapter 7 was bedside reading for the Galatian Christians, and that the two passages were saying the same thing? Surely not: because the letter to the Romans was not written, and may not have seen the light of day for another ten years. Well then, if the apostle had wanted us to think of the flesh as sinful and evil, why did he not say so?

Anyhow, all this has prompted scholars to search for a wider and better translation for *sarx*. They have come up with one. Could flesh signify 'what is merely human'?

Let us now sum up where we have reached. (i) In Galatians chapter 5, Paul is not exploring the inner life. Rather, he is trying to correct the lack of love in the church, the Christian family.[10] 'You are on the wrong road', he writes to the Galatians. 'You have forgotten where you began. Turn round and go back to that happy time when you were living and walking by the Spirit.' (ii) 'Sinful nature' may not be the best translation for *sarx*. Why not try 'what is merely human'? That might fit all the key passages. In his remarkable book *Obeying the Truth*, to which I am deeply indebted, Professor J. M. G. Barclay put it as follows: 'A much more satisfactory solution emerges if we take *sarx* as "what is merely human", and see its application to the works of the flesh … *in social* (my italics) rather than purely individualistic terms.'[11]

So let us see. If you have patiently followed the argument, a very different picture is beginning to emerge. Please look carefully at the diagram on the next page, and, remember that we are now thinking not about the individual, but about families, communities, and, if you like, (local) society, both non-

1

SELFISHNESS

Jealousy  Fits of rage  Drunkenness  Sexual immorality  and so on

2

Trustworthiness

Joy  Peace

LOVE

Kindness  Goodness

Self-control

and so on

Works of those who are 'merely human' or, rather 'less than human'

Fruit of the Spirit
The life of the fully human

Christian and Christian. This explains why *sarx* can be a threat although it has been crucified (Galatians 5:24). Paul is not thinking about an individual's 'physical being, or his lower nature, but with the influence of an era and its human traditions and assumptions … the real but intangible effects of social pressure and social expectations.'[12]

The first circle (under the grey umbrella, for *sarx* is an umbrella term) represents, say, the people of Iconium[13] in Galatia in AD 40, before Paul had told them about Jesus Christ. What were they like? Well, with prompting, no doubt, from the prince of darkness, these are the sorts of things that Paul says they got up to from *time to time*: sexual immorality, impurity, debauchery, idolatry, witchcraft, hatred, discord, jealousy, fits of rage, selfish ambition, dissensions, factions, envy, drunkenness and orgies. We are not told that they were *exceptionally* wicked. But they were certainly weak and vulnerable. After all, they were 'merely human'. I also need to emphasise the phrase from 'time to time', for I am not saying that every society apart from the Holy Spirit is as bad as it could be. That would be ridiculous. In society, Christian and non-Christian, God restrains evil in many ways; but before I come to that and leave 'mere human nature' behind, I would like to dig down a little further.

God created human nature. When he did so, he must have had Jesus in mind. Jesus, therefore, is the life-size portrait of what we should be like – perfectly normal, not super-human.

I am always impressed that the Gospel story tells us that 'Jesus came eating and drinking'. Because he was the Son of God, he didn't have a special diet[14] like many other so-called 'holy men'; he came eating and drinking – he was perfectly normal: he needed food, water and sleep, just as we do. It follows from this that to be 'in Christ,' and to be filled with his Spirit, is simply to be *fully human* – a glorious concept.

What, then, about *sarx* or flesh? Clearly, to be 'in the flesh' is to be *less* than human.[15] We are far weaker and far more vulnerable than we realise.

Turning back, now, to the grey umbrella and the circle below it, God, in his loving concern for the world, restrains evil in many ways. Every society has its laws. In the ninth century, King Alfred, famous for his burnt cakes, headed the laws of England with the Ten Commandments. He did it for a good reason. The Law, the judges and the police restrain evil. The Ten Commandments are 'a brilliant analysis of the minimum conditions on which … a nation can live a sober, righteous and civilized life.'[16] In the same vein, Abraham Lincoln once said, 'Let reverence for the law be sung by every mother to her child.' A child, lucky enough to have such a musical mother, grows up knowing what is right and wrong. Again, we all have a conscience, and the conscience teaches us something of the will of God. It is like a light that turns red when we tell a lie or steal. So, evil is curbed and restrained. Nevertheless, if for any reason, such restraints are removed, the evil in the grey circle may take over. It can happen suddenly and unexpectedly. Why is this? Let me explain a little more.

Eighty years ago, there was a master storyteller. He held children spellbound – and adults, too. His name was Hudson Pope. He was quite elderly when I heard him. He would say with a smile, 'I am going to tell you a story. It's a "pretend" story; and anything can happen in a pretend story. There was once a boy named Tom. He saved up his pocket money for many weeks, and on 1 November he walked down to the shops with his father, and spent it all on a large box of fireworks. When he got home, he went into the kitchen and put the box on a shelf above the stove. His mother noticed it. "Tom, what's in that box?" "Fireworks, Mummy." "Oh, are they?" said his mother, lifting her finger to make her point. "Take them out of the warm kitchen and put them in the shed at the bottom of the garden. Off you go – at once!" Now, as I said, anything can happen in a "pretend" story. As Tom was walking down the garden path, a squib poked its head out of the box, and said in a miserable voice, "Tom, why, are you putting me in a cold dark shed? I was comfortable in the kitchen, and I haven't done anything wrong." Tom looked at the squib. "I am sorry, squib, to treat you like this; but, you see, it's not what you've *done* that's the problem. The worry is not what you've *done*: it's what is *in* you." ' Hudson Pope would repeat those last words very slowly, 'it's what's *in* you'. Then he quoted the words of Jesus, 'From *in*side, out of men's hearts, come evil thoughts, sexual immorality, theft, murder, adultery, greed, malice, deceit, lewdness, envy, slander, arrogance and folly. All these evils come from *in*side and make a man "unclean".'[17] A little girl might say, 'Mr Pope, I don't know what all those long words mean.' There would be a pause before Mr Pope continued. 'No, you don't. *And I hope you never will.* But Jesus said that all these bad things were *in* us; and given temptation, the right circumstances, the wrong company, out they come.'

Only a children's story; and yet, at the climax of that story was a profound comment of Jesus on the human heart (the weak will we inherit from Adam). Once again, Jesus clarifies why we need a new nature – a nature born from above by the Holy Spirit. The comment explains why delightful, educated, civilised men and women – given the three conditions at the end of the story – can sometimes suddenly behave so badly. It also throws light on some of the darkest deeds in the history of the world: in Stalin's Russia or Hitler's Germany.

In 1914, Germany was wealthy, cultured, and the most highly educated country in the world. The Jews had helped to make her great, winning many Nobel prizes for her. A mere nineteen years later, Hitler embarked on the holocaust. 'It is still in many respects a mysterious event,' wrote Paul Johnson; 'not as regards the facts which have been documented in stupefying quantity, but as regards the causes.'[18] Johnson skilfully examines the reasons why and how this monstrous crime was hatched. They are many and complex. But Hitler's cruel plan would have made little headway if, in the early twenties – the years when the Nazis were rising to power – 'the restraints' had not collapsed. The rule of law failed. Judges let off lightly the ex-army thugs who were already murdering Jews. The university authorities were weak; they didn't stand up to the students who rioted against the Jews and forced many Jewish professors to resign and flee the country. By 1933, the whole nation knew that the Jews were being persecuted, and by 1939 it was clear that thousands were being murdered. But, with a few heroic exceptions, there was no protest. It was far too dangerous. People closed their eyes to what was happening. What could they do? If we had been in their shoes, what would *we* have done?

Anyhow, the three conditions were in place. (i) A diabolical temptation: the wealth of the Jewish community waiting to be seized. (ii) The right circumstances: the restraints had gone; no danger of being caught and punished. (iii) The wrong supportive company. There were the street-bullies, the Brownshirts, 500,000 strong, going about their ugly work quite openly; there were 900,000 in the SS alone; and there were 1,200,000 involved with the railways.

These all knew about the nightly trains, packed with Jews, speeding on their way to the death camps. The grey circle triumphed. What was *in* the unredeemed hearts of men, came out – murder. Six million murders.

Coming nearer home, a friend of mine was in Harrods when an IRA bomb exploded. As he hurried to the exit, he was startled and shocked to see well-dressed shoppers furtively slipping expensive clocks and other valuables into their carrier bags. Why had these prosperous members of the west London community taken to looting? In the smoke and confusion, they had calculated that the risk of being caught and disgraced was minute. Once again, 'restraints' had gone. There was the temptation to thieve. Others were doing it; so why not? Theft was in their hearts. And out it came.

Forgive me if I seem to be in danger of becoming the Revd Oozing Gloom. Our humanity, weak as it may be, is made in the image of God and is capable of producing great and beautiful qualities: a mother's love; the spirit of adventure that takes men and women to the moon; a long and blissful marriage; the courage that wins the VC; the affection and trust of a child; to mention but a few.

Equally, it is folly shining bright to forget what Jesus says about us, and to fail to learn the lessons of the grey circle.

Nevertheless, after remembering Hitler and Stalin, it is a joyous thing, and spiritually refreshing, to turn to an alternative society on offer – a community of people under the control and leadership of the Holy Spirit; see circle 2, under the yellow umbrella. What were *they* like?

Here is St Paul's proud answer. 'They love each other. They bring joy to each other. They live at peace with each other. They are patient with each other. They are kind to each other. They are good to each other. They are trustworthy. They are gentle with each other. They control themselves.'[19] This is not a complete list: Paul might have added other 'fruit,' such as 'they forgive each other, they are generous to each other,' and so on.

Now I would like to leave my yellow circle under its yellow umbrella on p.169 just as it is, because it so well illustrates the great difference between society 'in *sarx*' and society 'in the Spirit'. But I can't. It's an over-simplification. Attentive readers will remember that in chapter 3, p. 89, I drew attention to so-called vice lists in the New Testament, and I argued that when God transferred us into the kingdom of Jesus, we almost certainly took with us patterns of behaviour, memories, tendencies and habits that we had picked up in the kingdom of darkness. I suggested that you looked at these lists, and if, at any point(s), your conscience smote you, I encouraged you to take the rebuke seriously. First, by repenting, or as the original word really means, by changing your mind. For remember Charles Spurgeon's words:

Tis not enough to say, we're sorry and repent,
And then go on from day to day just as we
    always went.
Repentance is to leave the sins we loved before,
And show that we in earnest grieve by doing
    them *no more*.[20]

Second, after grieving and going to God for forgiveness, whatever you do, don't simply decide 'to try harder'. Ask God to fill you again with his Holy Spirit, and don't leave your knees until you are resting securely on his promise (see pp. 133–34). Then, and only then, are you empowered to fight the darkness and to drive the sin out of your life. And you can! And, if you do this at once (and, clearly, the apostles expected the first Christians to act promptly) it will spare you much grief and much trouble. If you look at the following page, you will see that I have modified the yellow circle to reflect these battles.[21]

We all begin life in circle 1. But we have to come out of circle 1 and enter circle 2. How does this great change take place? This is how St Paul describes it in his letter to the Colossians. '[God] has rescued us from the dominion of darkness [the grey circle] and brought us into the kingdom of the Son he loves'[22] [the yellow circle]. *It is God who has done it all* through the death and resurrection of Jesus Christ (see diagram on p. 49). Is Christ your Lord and Saviour? You say, 'Yes, indeed he is.' Then where are you in the diagram on p.169? And

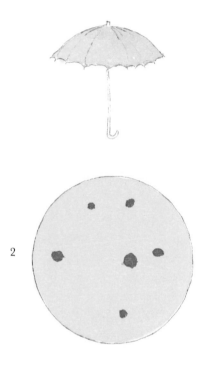

A great change has taken place – the golden circle; but there are still 'blots' – patterns of behaviour, bad memories, tendencies and so on that we have picked up in the kingdom of darkness. As the days go by, the Holy Spirit will make us aware of 'blots', often when we are praying and reading the Bible. Then, we must act at once.

where are you in the diagram on p. 180? I would ask you to pause, and to think carefully before you reply.

The answer, of course, is that on p. 49 you are on the right side of the great divide, in the green area. On p. 180 you are in the yellow circle. God himself has put you there. He has transferred you. Being transplanted from the grey circle to the yellow circle is like going to a new country. There is a new government, a new language, new customs, new neighbours, new friends – like moving from France to the UK, or from England to America. And the more clearly we see this wonderful truth, the more joyous will our Christian life be. When the devil shouts across the gulf, we will penetrate his disguise, and resist him until he flees. When he drops an evil thought into our mind, and then accuses us of being 'just the same as we always were', we will stand our ground. We will fight back, 'No, no, I am not in your dominion; I died with Christ. I am a new man, a new woman in Christ.' We will begin to laugh. After all, there is no reason why we should not catch *all* the flaming darts of the devil with the shield of faith.

You may ask, what then is the battle between 'flesh' and 'Spirit' in Galatians 5? If it is not an inner struggle, what is it? On the diagram, the question would be, 'How do the two circles regard each other?' (see the diagram p. 180).

The apostle gives his answer: 'The whole energy of merely human society,' he says, 'is set against the people of the Spirit … .'[23] In a word, the grey circle (aided and abetted, as I said earlier, by the prince of darkness) *dislikes* the yellow circle; and the yellow circle stands up to the grey circle and resists it. The grey circle doesn't mind too much if the yellow circle keeps quiet. But the more outspoken the yellow circle is, and the more it takes a clear stand against the behaviour of the grey circle, the deeper the dislike of the yellow circle will become. Is this not so?

'Works of the flesh'

'Fruit'

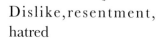

Dislike, resentment, hatred

Do you think that 'hatred' is too strong? A bit paranoid? Then see (right) what Jesus himself said, and don't be surprised when it happens.

Resistance, standing their ground in Christ, loving those in the grey circle but refusing to do what they do. 'If the world hates you, keep in mind that it hated me first' (John 15:18).

George, a schoolboy, becomes a Christian. The parents are distressed. The poor boy has become an extremist. What should they do? Is he drinking heavily? No. Is he on drugs? No. Has he become a recluse? No. Have the police called? No. So what's the problem? Well ... well ... he has chummed up with some other boys who go to church on Sunday evening ... it's so odd for a boy of his age ... inconvenient, too, when we want to go out as a family ... and he's actually reading a Bible.

The pressure is on and George knows it. His elder brother insists on calling him 'St George' and 'the vicar'. George laughs, but it's not easy. He is conscious of the resentment rising from the grey circle.

Tamsin sets out for university. She's a beautiful girl, and clever, too. But, oh dear, there is something different about her. She didn't get drunk in the first week. How odd! She won't sleep with her boyfriend. Why not? She's missing out on so much fun. She says she's a Christian. How quaint! How judgmental! What a pity.

The conflict is real. Tamsin feels it.

From studying the two circles, you might think that the best Christians would mind their own business, stay in their own shells and, as far as possible, keep away from 'merely human' society. That would be a great mistake. Paul saw the world in terms of two ages. First, there is the society and culture of the age people live in. That he calls 'this present age'. It's a way of thinking not unfamiliar to us. We talk about the Space Age, and we remember the swinging Sixties. It's the same idea. Sometimes, St Paul adds the word 'evil' – 'this present evil age';[24] and with good reason, when he saw what 'mere humans' got up to in the Roman empire. But, he says joyously, another, a much greater, age has dawned. It began with the coming of Christ to earth, his death, his resurrection and the pouring out of the Holy Spirit.

At present, these two ages overlap. And they will continue to do so until Christ returns. Then the present evil age will end.

Can we now see God's plan? On the one hand, we Christians are to renounce 'what is merely human' in society, with its base appetites and sinful desires. On the other hand, like God, we are to love those in the world.[25] We are to try to stay right in the middle of 'less than human society' in all its weakness and sinfulness. We are to be active in it. God, like a town planner, may well want to place us in some particularly dark and dangerous corner to be a lamp post there; or, to use us, like salt in the ancient world, as a refrigerator to stop society getting worse. Jesus put it perfectly when he said that his disciples were to be 'in' the world, but not 'of' the world.[26] St Paul goes on to say in Galatians chapter 6, 'I am crucified to the world, and the world is crucified to me.'[27] You may feel that his use of words is over-dramatic. Crucifixion is such a violent and painful word. Well, it may seem so in this country. But, do we not realise that *now*, in the twenty-first century, many men and women – from the day they are baptised – become 'a horror' to their family and closest friends? From then on their lives are at risk. That was true in the Roman empire, and it is true in much of the world today. It was certainly true for St Paul. Was he then playing to the gallery when he wrote that, in the eyes of the world, he was like a poor wretch hanging on a cross by the roadside?

This is hard. We are not '*less than* human', not even *merely* human; we are filled with the Holy Spirit. But we *are* still human – weak human beings. At times the prince of this world (the devil) will tempt us severely to behave 'in a less than human way'. For a time, some of us may even seem to go back into the grey circle. But we mustn't deceive ourselves. If we stay there, remove the nails, and make the grey circle our home even for a short time, we are in grave spiritual danger. We must cry out for help. We would badly need it.

If you have been able to follow what I have been trying to say so far, and are not confused at a deep level, you may be becoming aware that Paul's argument in Galatians sparkles in a new way. I must spend a little time in saying what I mean by this.

Being justified by grace, through faith, is still the bedrock on which the whole of the Christian life rests, and that is why the apostle fights for it in the first two chapters. But his chief concern in the letter begins at chapter 3, namely how to *maintain* the Christian life.

'Having begun *in the Spirit* ...', he says, 'why, oh why do you not *continue in the Spirit?*'

This is relevant today. When, as a young man of eighteen, I began my Christian life, I began very quietly. I trusted the wonderful promise of Revelation 3:20: 'Behold I stand at the door and knock. If any man hears my voice and open the door, I will come in, and will sup with him and he with me.' After a few weeks, I had no doubt that Christ had entered my life. I had feelings of peace and, at times, even of quiet joy. It was wartime, I was in the ranks of the Royal Air Force training to be a pilot, and I remember, vividly, discovering the words of Jesus in St John's Gospel, 'Truly, truly, I say to you, he who hears my word and believes on Him who sent me, *has* eternal life; he does not come into judgment, but *has* passed from death to life.' I realised, with quiet relief, that if my plane was shot down, or a bomb dropped on me, I would still be all right. (It is only in the assured peace of being joyfully ready to meet death that a man's whole personality is set free.) Life was tough; there were many temptations and my experience was uneven. Sometimes, I seemed to win, but often I lost. I suspected that this was the pattern of many of my Christian friends. You must not think that I am sad about those early days, or that I am critical of those who taught me so kindly and patiently. I am deeply grateful to them. They laid an excellent foundation. However, I was worried that often my experience did not match up with what I read in my New Testament. Where was the *'abundant* life' that Jesus promised? Why was I not being 'kept − *a bit more efficiently* − by the power of God'? Could I say that my life was 'holy and without blame'? Not really. Was I reading my Bible? Yes. Was I praying? Yes. Was I a secret disciple? No. Four years later, I returned to university. Before the term began, there was a three-day conference for Christians. The speaker[28] took as his theme Romans, chapter 6 linked with Galatians 2:20 (KJV) 'I am crucified with Christ, nevertheless I live,' and, in response to God's grace, I re-surrendered myself to Christ and I was filled with the Holy Spirit. It was an amazing experience and took me completely by surprise. I walked on air for many weeks. My Christian friends were pleased that I had returned from the RAF apparently in such good spiritual health, but nobody seemed to understand what was going on, nobody explained to me how this fitted in with the rest of the structure of the Christian life, and to what extent it could and should be maintained. The glowing awareness of God's presence gradually faded.

Today the situation is different. Many men and women, like the Galatians long ago, seem to begin their Christian life with a dynamic experience of the Spirit. They were not filled imperceptibly (either to themselves or to others), so, when St Paul speaks about God 'supplying the Spirit generously' it makes very good sense to them. Here are some of the things they say. 'God has washed me clean. He began at the top of my head, and finished with my feet' (a man). 'My whole body was bathed with bright light. Love flooded into me' (a woman). 'For the first time in my life I felt normal' (a man). 'I had a most powerful manifestation of God, and I saw that Jesus died for me' (a woman). 'I had to sit down. I began to cry and I could not stop. I knew that night that I had become a Christian' (a man). 'The power of God fell upon me. I collapsed into my chair. I received the gift of another language. At the end of the weekend, I was full of joy and love for everyone' (a man). There are endless stories like these. They remind us of what seems to have been normal in the early days of the church. Their 'experience of the Spirit was usually very vivid, an event often deeply moving and profoundly transforming, which the young Christians would have no difficulty in recalling'.[29]

Now I am not saying that Christians continue on an emotional 'high' for the rest of their lives. But when God intervenes and we discover something of the mighty power of the glorious third Person of the Trinity in our own experience, often in our own bodies, we never forget it. We are never the same. Paul knew this and his first readers knew it. (By the way, you must remember that the Christian Jews from Jerusalem were telling the Galatians, 'By all means believe in Jesus, but keep the law. If you give up the law, what is going to keep you out of mischief? You will never live holy lives, unless you try to keep the Jewish law.') To try to protect them from this nonsense, Paul had burst out at the beginning of chapter 3, 'O you dear idiots of Galatia ... surely you can't be so idiotic as to think that a man begins his spiritual life in the Spirit and then completes it by reverting to outward observances?'[30] So when later in the letter he wrote, 'Walk in step with the Spirit', they could not possibly have thought that Paul was preparing them – people of the Spirit – for 'a life of continuing frustration'.

Indeed, he goes on immediately to point out that the Holy Spirit is quite powerful enough to enable them to live continuously holy lives.

I now go back to what I said on at the beginning of this chapter (pp. 164–65). If the apostle had concluded his argument with what I have called 'the sad admission' – namely that, 'As a believer you will find yourself torn by conflicting desires and impulses, and your experience as a man of the Spirit in the flesh is one of continuing frustration' is he not flatly contradicting all that he has said since the beginning of Galatians chapter 3? He has destroyed his own case.

Well then, let us begin again. How did the Galatians understand the paragraph Galatians chapter 5, verses 16–21, and in particular 'the sad admission' at the end of verse 17?

I believe they read it like this. 'So I say, live by Spirit and you will *not* (a very strong 'not' in the original) gratify the desires of the grey circle.' Of course we won't. We have already come out of the grey circle, and taken a stand against much of what those in the grey circle get up to. So St Paul continues, 'Because the desires in the grey circle are against the desires in the yellow circle, and the desires in the yellow circle are against the desires in the grey circle.' Indeed they are! And here … wait for it … comes the so-called 'sad admission': 'so that you do not do what *you want*'.

The question that faces us is, 'What are these "wants"?' And if we have been swept along by the current of St Paul's argument, there can be only one answer. They must be *'merely human'* wants (perhaps with the devil behind them, see Event 2) which, from time to time, wink alluringly at the Christian from the shores of the grey circle, but to which the Spirit has said 'No'. The Galatians have indeed been 'called to be free', but the Spirit ensures that this is not carte blanche for doing whatever one wants'.[31] I would like to add that the only true freedom the Christian enjoys is to obey Christ. That is why I made no bones about saying so much about the lordship of Christ on pp. 137–39.

Now, if, for a moment, you accept that translation and you read through the passage again, you will see that it fits beautifully together. The Christian life is all grace and faith and the Spirit. We begin by faith in Christ crucified and God gives us his Spirit.[32] So we begin in the Spirit. And we continue in the Spirit, cooperating with him.

When we fail, we don't 'slug it out in the trenches'.[33] We confess our sin, then ask to be refilled with the

Spirit. And such is the power of the Spirit that we are absolutely safe without the help of the Law.[34] We won't chew each other up. We shall be so filled with the Spirit of love that we will voluntarily carry one another's luggage!

All this is very exciting. In the meantime, I have almost forgotten where I had got to. (i) The letter to the Galatians sparkles in a new way. (ii) Galatians Chapter 5 is no longer an obstacle to our interpretation of Romans 6. We must now turn to Romans, chapter 7.

# *Notes*

1. See introduction, p. 14.

2. Galatians 5:16, 17 (NIV).

3. Ephesians 6:16.

4. Galatians 5:17c.

5. James D. G. Dunn, 'Romans 7:14–25 in the Theology of Paul', *Present Truth Magazine*, Vol. 31, Article 8. See http://www.presenttruthmag.com/archive/XXXI/31-8.htm

6. Romans 6:14, KJV.

7. For example, 2 Corinthians 7:1, Ephesians 1:4, Cololssians 1:22, 1 Peter 1:15.

8. Gordon Fee, *God's Empowering Presence* (Hendrickson Publishers, 1994), p.388; Gk *epichoregeo*.

9. Galatians 5:13, 16, 17, 19.

10. Galatians 5:13, 15, 26

11. *Obeying the Truth* (Fortress Press, 1991), p.209

12. *Obeying the Truth*, p.213.

13. Now Konya, in the middle of Turkey.

14. It was said of one 'holy man' that it cost a great deal of money to keep him at the level of poverty to which he was accustomed.

15. I owe this definition, and the thought that lies behind the previous paragraph, to Dr Graham Tomlin.

16. Bishop Stephen Neill, *The Supremacy of Jesus* (Hodder & Stoughton, 1984), p.40.

17. Mark 7:21–23 (my italics).

18. Paul Johnson, *A History of the Jews* (Phoenix Press, 2001), pp.470, 498.

19. Galatians 5:22.

20. Cp. John 8:11.

21. Also I have found it helpful to choose the appropriate fruit of the Spirit (eg self-control) and to include prayer for the ripening of that fruit in my daily prayers.

22. Colossians 1:13.

23. A paraphrase of Galatians 5:17, based upon J. B. Phillips' translation. See also N. T. Wright on Colossians 2:11–12 (Tyndale, p.106) where he suggests that *sarx* might be translated 'family solidarity', together with his footnote on Romans 11:14 where *sarx* is translated 'my own people'.

24. Galatians 1:4.

25. The *world* is a technical word in John's Gospel. It does not mean the world as God created it; rather 'society apart from God'.

26. John 17:16.

27. Isaac Watts, I suspect, glimpsed this truth. In his hymn 'When I Survey the Wondrous Cross' there is a verse usually, alas, omitted in modern hymn books and here it is: 'His dying crimson like a robe/Spreads o'er his body on the Tree;/ *Then am I dead to all the world/* [Galatians 6:14] *And all the world is dead to me'.* 'The world' = society apart from God.

28. I even remember his name: The Revd E. J. H. Nash.

29. James D. G. Dunn, *Word Biblical Commentary: Romans 1–8* (Thomas Nelson, 1988), p. 328, commenting on 1 Corinthians 12:13.

30. J. B. Phillips' translation.

31. Professor John Barclay, *Obeying the Truth*, p. 115.

32. Galatians 3:1.

33. I owe this colourful phrase to Professor Gordon Fee.

34. Galatians 5:18.

## Chapter 9

# Things Hard to Understand: Part 2

R omans 7:14 onwards is a catalogue of misery and woe. Here are some quotations. 'All sorts of forbidden desires are aroused within me ... I realised that I was a sinner doomed to die ... I am sold into slavery with Sin as my owner ... for I really want to do what is right, but I can't. I do what I don't want to – what I hate ... I know I am rotten through and through' (*The Living Bible*). And much else; but that is probably enough to give you the flavour. Then from the lowest depth, and just before the sun shines out and the dark landscape is suddenly glorified in chapter 8, comes St Paul's dismal cry, 'What a wretched man I am!'

So we have to begin by asking the question, 'Who on earth does Romans 7:7–25 describe?' Is it Paul himself on a bad day? Is it an unbeliever? Or a baby Christian dirtying his nappy? Or is it Paul, the saint, with an awareness of sin that run-of-the-mill Christians like ourselves don't feel? Or is it a man under law – a woman governed by endless rules? Or is it every Christian? A good case can be put up for all these; and if you think about each one in turn, and imagine yourself in their shoes, you will, I think, be forced to say, 'It is *just* possible. Yes, in that situation, I *could* sometimes feel, "What a wretched man I am!"' That is why the passage is such a minefield. It *is* very difficult. If you say to me, 'I don't agree with what you are writing,' I shall not be surprised, and certainly not be upset. Any understanding I may have of the passage, I owe entirely to the prayers and hard work of others.

Very roughly, two views have been held about 'the wretched man'. Some learned scholars have thought that he represented the non-Christian world. Equally learned scholars have been convinced that he was a Christian. The argument has continued vigorously for two thousand years without making much progress. In the last century, some commentators began to feel that the above debate – is the wretched man a Christian or an unbeliever? – misses the whole point. So, there are these three parties. And, I assure you, brilliant saintly people of God are to be found in each one of them. Yet they disagree.

I must now pause to say something that I feel deeply. Christians can live above their doctrine. They can also, alas, live below their doctrine. Fortunately, God deals with us, not according to the correctness of our intellectual understanding, but according to the burning desires of our hearts.

The reason why the debate on Romans 7 generated so much heat was that the various opinions influence the way in which we, as Christians, think of ourselves. The picture opposite suggests one way, a way that is *not* recommended. I only include it because, alas, it is so common.

Does it matter if we think like this? Yes, indeed it does. There is a deadly danger that, at the moment of temptation, we fight *ourselves* instead of the real enemy. Let me try to explain.

The devil is a master of deception. He hides. We can't see him. But, as we know, he has access to our thoughts; so he drops a thought into our minds. The danger (particularly in an age that banishes the devil to the world of hobgoblins) is that we attribute the thought to our 'old nature'. 'I was born like that' we say to ourselves. 'My father enjoyed drinking, and probably drank too much, and I'm the same. But he had a good head, and so have I.' So we accept the thought. Then when we realise that we have had a drop too much, and are feeling woozy, we struggle with ourselves. 'Stop it!' we say under our breath. But it's too late. That way lies defeat. 'Desire when it has conceived gives birth to sin'.[1] And from the moment the thought was first dropped into our mind, to the moment our weak will said 'Yes', we never glimpsed the real enemy. The enemy was not a member of our family, nor our enjoyment of a

## *The Divided Heart*

This is *not* a good way to think of yourself:

glass of wine, nor our friends (though all these may have contributed), but the devil. Similarly, with other temptations, the real enemy is not our quick brain, nor our quick tongue, nor our sex drive, nor our healthy appetite, nor anything else, but the devil. And the devil is no paper tiger; he is mighty, violent, intelligent, a liar, and he can enter a man and even control him.[2] It is foolish to underestimate the devil.

In the Bodleian Library at Oxford, there is a portrait of the Puritan Dean of Christ Church, John Owen, which I often gaze at: his hair so black, his nose so long, his face so solemn. And perhaps, as he looks sternly at us above his preaching bands, we think, a trifle condescendingly, 'Thank God I am not one of his students. Poor man, has he not fallen into the very trap that the young Spurgeon escaped?' (see pp. 52–53). But then we read his works, and we rapidly revise our opinion; for we find John Owen describing his relationship with Jesus. What does he say about it? He says that he is 'sick with love' for his Saviour. Isn't that beautiful? It might be Bernard of Clairvaux.

What I am suggesting is that we may be forced to disagree at some points with great Christians of the past but, if there is bitterness in our disagreement, it would be sinful. They were struggling, as we are, to be true to Scripture. And if we disagree with them it is simply because, after hundreds of years of prayer and study, fresh light has fallen on a difficult passage, and this enables us to interpret it differently.

So what has changed? The third group, the more recent commentators (and I think that I think(!) that I have been convinced by them) suggest that St Paul, in a passage full of 'I's while never mentioning the Holy Spirit, is answering a question that must have been of agonising concern to Christian Jews. Let me put it like this. A devout Christian Jew in AD 54 might well have protested in some such words as these. 'Look here, I can't help feeling a sense of annoyance: God gave the Law to us through Moses. Keep my Law, he said, and you will have life. Break it, and you will have misery and death. We Jews tried hard to keep it. And, on the whole, we were pretty successful. The Law produced both a Temple that shone with the glory of God, and a kingdom (of David and Solomon) that left the Queen of Sheba breathless with admiration. Then we lost it all, and were punished by being dragged off to exile, just as Adam was expelled from the garden. Why? For our disobedience – for not keeping the Law properly. And now you Christians seem to be getting rid of the Law altogether. What on earth then was God's purpose in giving it to us in the first place?'

Paul's answer was this: 'God gave us Jews an immense privilege. He entrusted us with the Law, written not by some committee in the desert, but by his own finger. To keep the whole Law *outwardly* was no easy task, but not impossible.[3] Even at that level, the Law protected us from endless evils, like a good childminder keeping her young charges from harming themselves. That is why the Queen of Sheba was "blown away" by what she saw when she visited Jerusalem. However, to keep the Law *inwardly – in thought –* well, that is a different matter, as I, and everybody else, discover. We were caught out by the tenth commandment – "You shall not covet." Coveting is hidden, you know: it takes place only in the thoughts, and we found that, being *"in Adam"* as we were, our thoughts were out of control.

Fortunately, the Queen couldn't read King Solomon's thoughts. She might have had a shock. Indeed, in a funny way, the Law, good and holy as it is, stirred us up to sin. At the end of the day, we Jews were faced with a horrifying fact. With all our privileges, with all our efforts, and with all our claims, we were really no better than honest pagans.[4] The more we hugged the Law, the more we became conscious of how *sinful* we were, both outwardly and *inwardly*.'

'So to return to the question, "Why did God give us the Law?" My answer is, "first, to restrain us from sin until Jesus came: but also that God wanted one nation in the world, the Jews, to realise what a terrible problem evil is, and how helpless even the best of people are in the face of it."'

But of course Paul didn't stop there. In his summary of the chapter, he cries out first, 'Who will deliver me …?' Followed by the joyous shout, 'Thanks be to God, through Jesus Christ.' Only God could solve the problem, through the cross and the Spirit. God came himself. He came in weak, human, Jewish, Messianic flesh, and became the perfect sacrifice for the sin of the world. Thus, not only a Jew, but an Iranian, or a Nepali, or an American, or a Swede or even an Englishman, *'in Christ'* is rescued from being *'in Adam'*, becomes a true child of Abraham, and, filled with the Holy Spirit, can resist the devil's temptations successfully and live a life that delights God. Indeed God's purpose for us is even more glorious; to become like Jesus, and to bring his love to a needy world.

Deliverance is available now, in this life. Jesus the Saviour has come. God's ancient promise to Abraham, 'In you shall all the nations of the earth be blessed', is coming true.

If this brief résumé is correct (at least in general outline), Romans 7, however important in clarifying God's eternal purposes for the coming of the gospel, was never intended to be a guide to the inner life of the Christian. And, therefore, although we may admire distinguished Christians of earlier centuries in their struggles to be true to Romans 7,[5] and indeed rejoice that, by God's grace, their lives often exceeded their doctrine, nevertheless we must acknowledge that sometimes they were wrong. They misunderstood the purpose of the passage. Paul is not describing some never-ending tension in the Christian's heart. He is addressing a different question – why God gave the Law to the Jews.

Therefore neither Romans 7, nor Galatians 5, is any longer a barrier to our interpretation of Romans 6. And chapter 6 recovers its rightful place. It stands at the centre of the most important doctrinal book of the New Testament as the Magna Carta of the Christian life.

# *Notes*

1. James 1:15, RSV.
2. These are Dr Michael Green's headings for his description of the devil in his splendid study, *I Believe in Satan's Downfall* (Hodder and Stoughton, 1981), pp.49 ff.
3. See the claims of the rich young ruler in Mark 10:20, and of St Paul in Philippians 3:6.
4. Cp. Ovid: 'Video meliora proboque, Deteriora sequor'; I see and approve of what is better, I follow what is worse. Met. vii.19.
5. For further study of Romans chapter 7, I warmly recommend Tom Wright, *Paul for Everyone Romans Part 1: Chapters 1–8*. Tom Wright was formerly Bishop of Durham, and is now Research Professor of the NT and early Christianity at St Andrew's University. But it is still a difficult and complex chapter and I suspect that 'Everyone' in Durham and St Andrew's must be brainier than 'Everyone' in other parts of the country!

## Chapter 10

# A Vision for Life

Is it possible to live a holy life, a useful life, pleasing to God? Yes, it is. It will not be easy; nonetheless, it *is* possible: if, and only if, we rely totally on the grace and goodness of the Lord. Looking back over his early years, St Paul put it like this: 'I persecuted the church'.[1] (That was a bad start for an apostle-to-be; it could scarcely have been worse.) However, shortly after his meeting with Jesus, he saw that the old Saul, Saul the persecutor of Christians, had been crucified with Christ, and that now he was a new man, Paul – a man who loved Christians. So he continues, 'But, by the grace of God, I am what I am, and his grace to me was not without effect. No, I worked harder than all of them.' Then he stops, and adds, quickly, 'yet *not I*, but the grace of God that was with me.'

Do you see? In one breath, he is saying, 'Yes, I have travelled all over the Roman empire. I have written endless letters. I have prayed for many hours. I have suffered. I have worked harder than any of my colleagues.' 'I, I, I.' Then, in the next breath, he is saying, 'It wasn't me at all. It was *God*: *God* leading me, *God* protecting me, *God* prompting me, *God* working through me.'

In that passage, St Paul is writing about his career. And the same is true of Christian character. For example, he urges the Christians at Philippi, '*work out your salvation with fear and trembling*'.[2] (By now, I am sure you realise that there is nothing passive about the Christian life. We are not wafted to heaven.) Yet, you might think from those two words, 'work out' that it is all up to *us*: our hard thought, our hard choices, our hard reading, our hard work. But in the very next breath, he adds, 'for it is *God* who works in you to will and to act according to his good purpose.'

I like the following quotation. 'The glorious paradox is that the more *the Spirit* [my italics] is at work the more *the human will* is stirred up: [enabling it] to think things through, to take free decisions, to develop chosen and hard-won habits of life ... to exercise moral muscle; knowing that one is doing it oneself, *and* that the Spirit is at work within.'[3] And I will add:

> The servants of Jesus Christ,
> In the will of God,
> With the Word of God on their lips,
> Empowered and led by the Spirit of God,
> And there are no limits.

## *Believing pages*

A life pleasing to God is impossible apart from being born from above. So we must begin there.

A new creation

John 3:5–6; Corinthians 5:17

Always *begin* with God's grace; what he has done. Don't forget to *pass through* the promises to God himself, and express your love to him. And, of course, vary your prayer to God the Father, God the Son, and God the Holy Spirit:

> *Heavenly Father, I believe that I am a new creation in Christ Jesus. Thank you so much. Amen.*

> *'Therefore, if anyone is in Christ, he is a new creation; the old has gone, the new has come.'*
> 2 Corinthians 5:17

*Father, I believe that by the power of the Holy Spirit, and in your name, I can overcome the temptations of the devil. Thank you. Amen.*

*'Resist the devil and he will flee.'*
James 4:7

Spiritual life begins with the new birth. But then there should be steady growth. Indeed, there is always room for growth. 'Don't curse the blossom because it is not yet the fruit, or the fruit because it is not yet ripe' (John Fletcher of Madeley, 1725–1789).

Fruit of the
Holy Spirit
Mature in
Christ

Galatians 5:22; 2 Corinthians 5:14–15

*Father, I believe that the Holy Spirit is changing me, making me mature, and enabling me to know you better. Thank you so much. Amen.*

*'We ... reflect as in a mirror the splendour of the Lord; thus we are transfigured into his likeness, from splendour to splendour.'*
2 Corinthians 3:18, NEB

*Father, I believe that, as I work with you, the Holy Spirit will give me his graces – his fruit – to make me like him, and his gifts to help me to serve him. Thank you. Amen.*

Read and re-read Ephesians 3:14–21. Also Ephesians 4:13.

In the New Heaven and New Earth

*'When [Christ] appears, we shall be like him, for we shall see him as he is.'*
1 John 3:2

Heavenly Father, I believe that, one day, we shall stand before your throne, and worship and serve you perfectly; and, then, you will 'wipe every tear from our eyes'. Thank you so much. Amen. (Revelation 7:9–17.)

Father, we adore you. Jesus, we adore you. Spirit, we adore you. Alleluia! Amen.

## A prayer for perseverance, based upon 1 Corinthians 15:56

Heavenly Father, throughout my life, make me steadfast, immovable; and, in the power of the Holy Spirit, always abounding in the work of the Lord Jesus. I ask this in his name, and for his glory. Amen.

## St Paul's prayer

Now to him who is able to do immeasurably more than all we ask or imagine, by the power which is at work within us, to him be glory in the church by Christ Jesus, throughout all ages, world without end, Amen. (Ephesians 3:20–21.)

# *Notes*

1. 1 Corinthians 15:9–10.
2. Philippians 2:12–13 (my italics).
3. Tom Wright, *Justification* (SPCK, 2009), p.164.

## Chapter 11

# Introduction Concluded

You may be surprised that this chapter is headed 'Introduction Concluded'. You were expecting 'Summary' or 'Epilogue'. But I chose this heading for a good reason. The *whole* book, the *whole* diagram is only a beginning, only an introduction. Hopefully we have studied the diagram and have understood the five Events. Let me then remind you again of George Herbert's lines:

A man who looks on glass
On it may stay his eye;
Or, if he pleaseth, through it, *pass*
And then the heaven espy.

Herbert is, of course, making a protest against rapid, superficial reading. More than that, he is telling us that intellectual understanding is not enough. At each step of the way, we need to pray earnestly, and to hold on to the promises until those unforgettable moments when we 'pass through' the diagram, and meet with, and are blessed by, God the Father, God the Son and God the Holy Spirit.

*Then* we are equipped to live the Christian life.

In the great outpouring of the Holy Spirit recorded in the Acts of the Apostles, the first believers, I suspect, discovered all this within a few days. They repented. They believed. They went down to the river (or a bowl of water was produced). They received 'the outward and visible sign' of having died with Christ and having been buried with him in baptism. They were carried across the gulf. They rose in Christ to a new place of life as they joined God's people, the body of Christ, waiting to welcome them on the riverbank. And if they had not already been drenched with the Spirit, the church prayed for them and laid hands on them. It all happened within a short space of time.

I want to add one thing more. The diagram is easy to remember, and conveniently knits together the five, life-transforming spiritual blessings offered to us by Jesus. In conversation with friends, I have many a time sketched it on the back of an envelope, and used it to give a fifteen-minute explanation of these wonderful doctrines. One verse for each point is enough, sometimes concentrating on, say, two of the five points, and skipping over the rest. I jot down the references as we go along. God often blessed these conversations and I hope that the book will be used in this way as well.

In her book, *Eats, Shoots, & Leaves*,[1] Lynne Truss muses on the use of the ellipsis (or …) in writing. She points out that millions of paperbacks, on sale at railway stations, traditionally end with three dots. 'At long last Gary was back with Margot. He swept her off her feet. It began to snow. But she was only conscious of his strong arm around her shoulder. She buried her face in the rough, black leather of his motorcycle jacket. "I will never doubt you again," she murmured … .'

What do these three dots mean? Lynne suggests that they are shorthand for 'Conjure up the picture. Use your imagination. Work it out for yourself.' It's easy enough. Gary and Margot married and lived happily ever after.

What next? Now you must use your prayerful, scripturally instructed imagination! Ahead lies the adventure of loving God, trusting him, obeying him, serving him and others; great friendships, opposition, suffering, fulfilment, battles, joys …

# *Notes*

1. Lynne Truss, *Eats, Shoots & Leaves* (Profile Books Ltd, 2003), p.167.

*Appendix 1*

# How to Explain the Diagram to a Friend

## Suggested directions

· Sit side by side, so that you can both see the diagram as it builds up. Look at the verses from the New Testament together. Probably one is enough for each point. Choose the one you like most!

· (a), (b), (c) etc. refer to the explanation of the opposite page.

· In practice, I develop *one* basic diagram [i.e. *see* (a) below] making the drawing as large as the paper allows. I place (b) on top of (a), adding the cross and Romans 5:1; then (c) on top of (b) and so on. The final picture is a mess – but don't worry. It is perfectly clear and understandable if you have been drawing it together. As soon as you feel sure that (b) is understood, move on to (c).

· The drawings we have just seen look complicated. In fact they are simple. You will easily master them.

· On each new drawing, *the additions* are in red, but I have kept the cross red throughout to remind us of the centrality of the cross. Normally, I use a black pen or a sharp pencil.

(a) Draw the diagram quickly, about a third of the way down the paper. This will leave room for additions *above* the diagram. The size of an envelope is sufficient, though A4 would be ideal. As you draw, say with a smile, 'This is the Good News!'

Then say: 'The 1, 2, 3, 4, 5 are five historical Events linked with the death and resurrection of Jesus.

1) He died.

2) He died and was buried.

3) God raised him to new life.

4) He ascended.

5) He poured out the Holy Spirit.'

Tied in with each Event is a spiritual blessing. (See p. 12 for further material. Don't mention chapters 6–9. Keep it simple!)

(b) Point to the first Event 1, which is the cross. Jesus *died* for me and I am forgiven: or even better, I am justified. Romans 5:1. (See page 19.) This is the astonishing fact

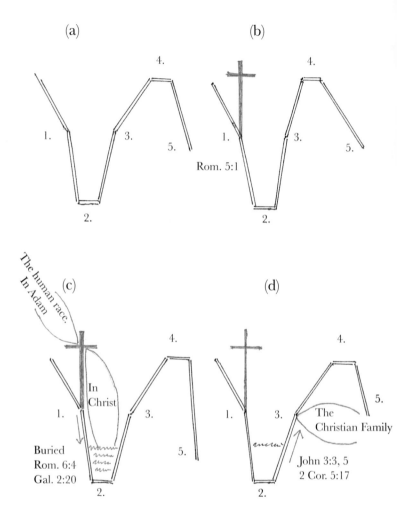

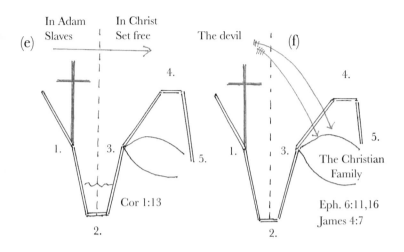

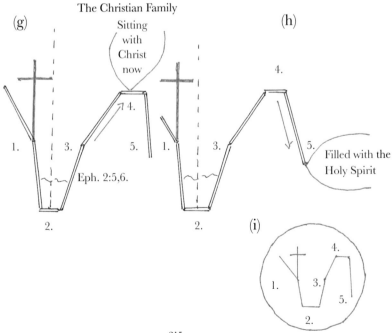

that, because, and only because, I have put my trust in Christ, God declares me righteous in his sight. Having explained this, I say (again, always with a smile): 'You *do* believe this, don't you?'

(c) Point to Event 2, and draw the fresh red material. So far, we have said, 'Christ died *for* me.' But often the New Testament puts if differently. St Paul writes that 'we died *with* Christ', and were buried *with* him. Romans 6:4,6; 2 Corinthians 5:14; Galatians 2:20. How so? Because when we put our trust in Christ, we become *one* with him. (Compare sugar in a cup of tea – see p. 40.) St Paul is shocked his readers didn't seem to *know* this. 'Don't you know?' He asks in astonishment. So if we are 'in Christ', what happened to Jesus happened to us. When he died, we died; when he was buried, we were buried – dramatised in baptism. This is how God sees us. This is how we are always to think of ourselves. (See pp. 46–47, and 56–62.) We might add, smilingly, 'Do *you* know this? More than that, do you *believe* it?'

(d) Point to Event 3. Happily, we don't remain in the grave. God raised Jesus from the dead, and we rise 'in him' to a new plane of life. John 3:5; 2 Corinthians 5:17. Moreover we find ourselves in the Christian family – with many new brothers and sisters who will love and support us (see p. 76).

(e) Draw in the divisions of the diagram – the dotted line. We have been taken from one side of the diagram to the other. Colossians 1:13. No longer are we 'in Adam', 'slaves', under the power of the devil. Now we are 'in Christ', born from above, children of God and set free from the power of sin. We are on the right side of the diagram. We shall never go back.

(f) Draw in the arrows from the devil to the Christian family. For (and this is *very* important) as long as we live, the powers of darkness will attack us and tempt us. Ephesians 6:11f. But we can block every arrow. Throughout our life on earth, we are at war with the powers of darkness. But this is a battle which, by God's grace, we can win! Luke 4:74, 75. How? Matthew 16:22. Tell the devil to be gone, in Jesus' name. And go on commanding him to leave you. James 4:7. He *must* go, if you persist.

(g) Point to Event 4. God doesn't stop when he brings us to life. Jesus ascended, and we ascend in him and sit with him. We are very close to him, and that is how God always sees us. Ephesians 2:5, 6. Do you believe this? Is this how you think of yourself? Sitting with Jesus? If we have grasped what Jesus has done for us in Events 1–4, our hearts will be singing! It is entirely God's goodness and grace.

(h) Point to Event 5 when Jesus poured out the Holy Spirit at Pentecost. We can say, 'God wants to fill *you* with his Holy Spirit. Make sure that Jesus is your Lord' (Acts 10:36). Then ask, and trust God's promise: 'He will give' (Luke 11:13). (See pp. 128–29.)

(i) Finally draw a circle round the complete Diagram to show that these five blessings equip us to live the Christian life. I suspect that, in the early church, people grasped them at their baptism, or shortly after. I have often found that, by this time, the friend to whom I am speaking is deeply interested. If so, you may like to suggest Alpha if they have not already done the course. Or you may feel it right to pray for the fullness of the Spirit at once, having looked at such passages as Acts 2:1–4; 8:17; 9:17; 10:44ff.

Printed in Great Britain
by Amazon